ATLANTIC OUTPOSTS

Harry Thurston

Pottersfield Press
Lawrencetown Beach, Nova Scotia

To the people of The Outposts who made me welcome
& who shared their lives

Copyright 1990 Harry Thurston

Canadian Cataloguing in Publication Data

Thurston, Harry, 1950-

 Atlantic outposts

 ISBN 0-919001-63-7

1. Atlantic Provinces --Description and travel.
2. Atlantic Provinces --Social life and customs.
I. Title

FC2004.T48 1990   971.5'104   C90-097626-8
F1035.8.T48 1990

Cover Photo of Mike and Ida Walsh in front of their home in Petit
Forte, Newfoundland by Stephen Homer.

*Printed in Canada on Europa 5 acid-free paper that contains 50%
recycled fibre and 5% deinked fibre.*

Published with the support of The Canada Council and The Nova
Scotia Department of Tourism and Culture

Author acknowledgements appear on page 192.

Contents

Gulf of

St. Lawrence

Atlantic Ocean

A. Anticosti Island
B. Advocate Harbour
C. Petit Forte
D. Cut Throat Island
E. Tatamagouche
F. McNutt Island
G. Bridgewater
H. Greenwich

I. River Hebert
J. Big Tancook Island
K. Springhill
L. Mooseland
M. Millstream
N. Dalhousie
O. Grand Manan
P. Sable Island

PREFACE

I was born an Atlantic Canadian and have lived all but two of my forty years in my native Nova Scotia. I confess to an almost congenital attraction to this place washed by the sea, which may explain why, like many other Atlantic Canadians, I simply could never bring myself to leave.

However, in the last decade, through my work as a journalist, I have travelled the length and breadth of Atlantic Canada, from the northernmost community in Labrador to Nova Scotia's easternmost domain, Sable Island. I have sought out backwoods settlements, isolated stretches of coastline, and barren rocks detached from the mainland and most people's itineraries. Always content at some distance from the centre — just as Atlantic Canada is distant from the centre of the country — I have set out happily for these places perched precariously on the rim of the continent, at the edge of the eastern ocean which gives the region its name.

However, I cannot claim that I systematically endeavoured to explore the many nooks and crannies of Atlantic Canada, or to bridge its far-flung outposts.

My journey began, inadvertently and inauspiciously, 2500 feet underground in a damp, cramped and accident-prone coal mine in River Hebert, Nova Scotia. As the coal car careened wildly, deeper and deeper into the black earth, I travelled back in time, through both geological ages and human history. What I found at the bottom of the mine was a working world like ones in England and France condemned outright by Dickens and Zola a century before. A way of life had survived in this outpost of the New World virtually unchanged since the 18th century. I came to the surface with a thin expose and never-to-be-forgotten images of men who literally seemed to be bearing the world on their shoulders.

"Mining A Thin Seam Wasn't God's Idea" appeared in the new regional magazine, *Atlantic Insight*. It marked the beginning of a career in the magazines, a career that has given me, as its greatest benefit, an opportunity to explore the part of Canada I call home. And so I found myself bobbing around on boats and travelling the region's byways to unlikely destinations like Mooseland, Advocate Harbour, Petit Forte and Cut Throat Island, heeding a siren call, at once harsh and seductive as the Babel of a seabird colony.

Besides geography, the one single thing that ties together these travels and the stories that came of them is the relationship of the people I met to the land and the sea around them — to their environment. All the stories collected here are about rural society in which it is still important to have a working relationship with one's surroundings. In Atlantic Canada many people have persisted in their traditional pursuits of work and life on the land and water, in the woods and mines — despite the forces of the 20th century that have conspired to steal away their livelihood and their culture. And it is these people whom you will meet: farmers, miners, fishermen, woodsmen, women and children. Together they make up the tiny communities that nestle in our coves, on islands or in the hinterland to which Atlantic Canadians have generally turned their backs. In fact, most of us now live in cities, but our ties and our traditions still reside in the outlying communities, "the outposts," as I call them.

By definition an outpost is "a settlement on the border or frontier of a country." Often it is used in a pejorative sense to signify a backwater, an undesirable destination where you would be loath to find yourself. Although I do not load the word with such meanings, it is true that those places at a far remove from the centres of power have been marginalized, economically and culturally, by the overriding concerns of urban society. And the experience of people living quite literally on the edge continues to be given short shrift.

In the outposts I found the keepers of tradition. In my opinion, their usefulness has not been outlived. In fact, it seems to me that we are in even greater need of the old ways as we face up to the consequences of our actions in this century. The outposts are repositories of important knowledge, ways of being based on time-proven methods.

There I listened to and recorded the thoughts and feelings of those who have chosen to avoid the mainstream, people like the residents of the tiny Newfoundland outpost of Petit Forte who simply refused to go when the government bullied them to resettle

6

to "growth centres;" and the proud island dwellers of Grand Manan, New Brunswick, who think of their tide-bordered rock as a country all its own. I have joined an Inuit family living off the land on the forbidding Labrador coast, as their ancestors did long before Cartier cruised by, tossed off his infamous epithet, "the land God gave to Cain," and began the extractive cycle of exploitation on this continent. I have shared the pitching deck of a Georges Bank scallop dragger with the men who, by dint of their labour, secure the margins of the country. I have admired the moral courage of loggers, housewives and farmers engaged in battles to save their birthright of forest and field from the dubious forces of progress. And I have listened to and learned from the reflections of the women and men who quietly follow the old ways — cutting in sauerkraut, separating cream on the farm, teaming oxen, keeping sheep on islands — because for them there is pleasure and dignity in simply doing something right.

By keeping alive the ways of the past, people in the outposts have forged a vital link with our traditions and, at the same time, fostered a sense of continuity. More than anything else, this connection to our common heritage accounts for the regional identity that people feel so strongly here. The belief in ourselves as a people possessed of collective memory has been critical to our survival during the hard times that have been so stubbornly persistent in Atlantic Canada.

It seems to me now that I undertook these stories (this journey) in an attempt to reconnect myself, and hopefully others, with the people and the places which together carry forward a truly maritime spirit. I think that I found something akin to that, harboured in the special places of the Atlantic coast — "The Outposts" — and in the hearts of the people who call them home.

I. ROAD TO THE OUTPORTS

"Road To The Outports" describes two isolated communities, one in Newfoundland and another in Nova Scotia. What these widely separated communities share is the unlikely distinction that neither should exist. Both might have disappeared from maps and memories long ago, if it hadn't been for the determination of people to stand together against the outside forces of change.

The outport of Petit Forte (which one well-travelled Newfoundland editor called "the tiny perfect place") resisted efforts by the Newfoundland government to resettle it, lock, stock, and barrel, to a so-called "growth centre." It stood, as its French name suggests, "small but strong" against the powers which rationalized that the future would be better if people left behind their stages and homes close to the traditional fishing grounds along the Newfoundland coast. More than 200 outports did resettle but the residents of Petit Forte believed their life and the life of their children could be just as good if they stayed — and they're glad they did. "Now it's better than ever," one resident told me.

Similarly, the residents of Advocate Harbour, one of Nova Scotia's most isolated communities, pulled together when foreign interests had depleted their traditional resource base of the fishery and forests. By helping each other through hard times, as their ancestors had done, they re-invented the means of building a future for their community. As I write, Advocaters are developing strategies to maintain control over the area's last natural resource, its beauty, by building a wilderness park at Cape Chignecto, the magnificent headland that cradles them.

So often the media leads (or should I say misleads) us to believe that Atlantic Canada survives only because of the largesse of the rest of the country, that somehow people here have lost the will to help themselves. These two communities give the lie to this myth.

OUTPORT RENAISSANCE

There is no road into Petit Forte. Rounding the light at Easter Point, the red roof of the church draws the eye toward the inlet where the community is sequestered. The mile-long harbour faces south and is enclosed by the calipers of a rugged and barren range of mountains. It is not until you pass the natural breakwater of Hayden's Point that you view the village in its entirety; at the water line, the sombre-coloured fish stores propped on weathered and spindly spruce pole wharves called stages; the houses in a semi-circle behind, by contrast white and trimmed in Christmas colours, but also erected on spruce pylons, levelled and facing the sea. This is "The Harbour" and it sits in the lap of a precipitous bluff, simply called "The Look-Off." From its peak, on a clear day, you can see the breadth of Placentia Bay to the Cape St. Mary's headland, some 40 miles away. This morning, fog was hanging on the mountaintops in billows backlit by the sun. Petit Forte was illuminated in the deceptively intense light that filtered through its prisms.

Ten years ago, Petit Forte's future was shrouded in uncertainty and the face it presented was considerably less bright, as Newfoundland's notorious resettlement programme threatened to empty another outport harbour.

At first sight, the peacefulness of the place masked its current vitality. The sleepy appearance was heightened because it was noon — the men were at sea, the women and children in their houses. Even the stages where the old men busy themselves were idle. As we drew opposite the public wharf, Billie Synard wheeled sharply to port and cut the engine at precisely the same moment, so that we drifted to a dead stop at the stage ladder.

Petit Forte lies at the mouth of Paradise Sound, an arm of Placentia Bay which cuts deeply into the eastern shore of the Burin Peninsula. On the two-hour trip from its head at Monkstown, I saw only one place where Billie Synard's 40-foot longliner could put in along the fjord-like coastline. A stream divided a thin strip of beach, and over the eons had cut a gulch through the mountains which flank both sides of the sound. At the crest of the beach was an acre or so of grass, where a handful of houses might have clustered, though nothing man-made remained to confirm that this was ever so. I pointed out the haven to Billie Synard. He cast his quick blue eyes from the wheelhouse. "Darby's Harbour," he shouted above the inboard diesel's steady din. After that, wherever I saw a clearing carved out among the alder, blueberry and spruce, I felt that it was safe to assume that people once wrested a living there. It seems that on "The Rock," as Newfoundlanders affectionately call their island, man must settle for a landfall, a place to rest between the sea which provides for him and the land which broods at his back.

When Newfoundland joined Confederation in 1949, many of its 1,500 rural communities were located on islands or along inaccessible reaches of its 10,000-kilometre coastline. These were the outports. Life was based on salt sun-cured cod, as it had been since the first colonists followed the excursions of Basque and Bristol fishermen who had harvested the riches of the Grand Banks as early as the 15th century.

Throughout Canada, the post-War period was marked by a rural-to-urban population drift. In Newfoundland, however, the phenomenon took place on a community-wide scale. In 1953, Premier Joey Smallwood undertook what has become known as the resettlement, or centralization, programme. As the cost of providing services to many outports was considered prohibitive, entire remote communities were relocated to government-approved "growth centres." The programme continued until the early 1970s. More than 200 outports were evacuated, but far fewer than the original government goal of 600. Some planners conceded that the mass rural depopulation programme would work to the detriment of many adults, but justified it in terms of the potential benefits to their children. For the first time, a generation of Newfoundlanders was to have access to modern education facilities and alternatives to a life of fishing.

All regions of Newfoundland were affected by resettlement, but none more profoundly than the Burin Peninsula. Boot-shaped like Italy (though of a less foppish turn), the Burin juts out into the Atlantic from the southwest corner of the island. Off its toe lie the islands of St. Pierre and Miquelon, the last vestiges of France's New

10

World empire. The Burin's proximity to the Grand Banks attracted settlers to the many islands and snug harbours along its ragged coast. The harsh and lonely environment bred a people whose life Newfoundland novelist Harold Horwood has described as "hard, cruel and dangerous, with limitless scope for heroism and resourcefulness." Resettlement displaced them to growth centres like Marystown (population 5,915), which offered employment in the fish processing plant and shipyard, and the amenities rural Canadians everywhere have come to expect of a service town.

Petit Forte, however, refused to be rationalized, cajoled or lured into oblivion. It stood, as the origin of its French name suggests, "small but strong" in the midst of a sea change of events.

"Resettlement was a mistake; it didn't make the country better," Mike Walsh says with an authority befitting a man older than the century. Although he thinks joining Confederation was the right move, for Mike and many like him, "the country" is, and always will be, Newfoundland. He introduces me as "the gentleman from the Dominion of Canada" to his wife.

Mike and Ida Walsh's house stands at the bottom of the harbour. Like an elderly statesman, it seems to greet and bid farewell to all visitors to Petit Forte. It is the paragon of a type: a two-storey, square structure with a shed roof — no frills except for the white picket fence that sets it off.

Mike is the patriarch of Petit Forte, and at 87 is fit enough to have roofed his house last summer. He believes that resettlement put many people of his generation in the grave before their time. He remembers a trip on the coastal boat, which makes a weekly run along Newfoundland's south coast between Argentia and Port-aux-Basques. That day, an old woman embarked at Red Island. She was leaving her lifetime home to resettle in Placentia, a town of 2,209, on the Avalon Peninsula. "I thought she was going to sink the boat from crying — it's sentimental stuff but it's true, boy."

After World War II, overseas demand for salt fish fell off dramatically, and prices plummeted to as low as $1.25 per quintal (112 pounds dry weight). It is no wonder that some welcomed resettlement, if only as a chance to get clear of the fishery.

"There were a lot of people moving out," Alfred Pearson remembers. "There was nothing to be done here, only go fishing."

However, you need only experience the desolation of one of the abandoned communities — collapsed roofs, black-eyed windows

11

staring vacantly out to sea, the look of a place that has been bombed out or ravaged by plague — to understand the bitterness that many outport Newfoundlanders still bear against the programme.

Despite my outlander status, I soon felt at home at Eugene and Geraldine Jones', and became accustomed to the constant crackle of the Citizens' Band radio. The boats clear the harbour before dawn and may not return until after dark. CB radios connect the fishermen to their families and to one another. The set might bring mundane news from "The Jiggin' Cove" — "The squids was jiggin' when we first got here, but they're not jiggin' at all now" — or a drama that threatens to bring life to everyone's worst fears, as happened on my last day in Petit Forte: "She won't sink altogether, will she?" came a woman's plea. Eugene was one of those who helped tow Albert Heffernan's burning longliner into the safety of her home harbour of South East Bight.

Eugene says nothing of the exploit when he returns home. A man who spends the best part of his days on the water knows well that the spectre of drowning is constantly leering over his shoulder, and that he can't afford bravado, certainly not for the benefit of strangers. The work is inherently dangerous and necessarily hard, but not so hard as it used to be, when men shipped off St. Mary's and the Labrador coast in schooners and handlined all day from dories.

I was surprised at the size of the boats used by the Newfoundland fishermen today. Most fish from open punts, which average 25 feet in length, small boats compared to the Northumberland Strait and Cape Island models preferred by Nova Scotian inshore fishermen, and seemingly fragile craft, considering they are fishing in North Atlantic waters.

Squid jigging is an institution in Newfoundland. Many fishermen still use trawl lines, and you need squid to bait the trawl hooks. Squid jigging, as anyone will tell you, can be one of two things: boring or dirty.

The two nights I went out, the squid were not jigging. For two hours, we sat bobbing the jigger, wearing the scar made by the jigging line deeper into the boat's gunnels. It's like in the famous A.R. Scammel song: "There's some standin' up and there's some lyin' down; While all kinds of fun, jokes and tricks are begun, As they wait for the squid on the squid jiggin'ground."

It is best to take along a bottle of beer, an illegal act, but one of the freedoms outport Newfoundlanders enjoy and would be loath to relinquish. Like all refuse, beer bottles are unceremoniously pitched into the sea. "Let her go, boy," I was admonished, when caught trying to stow a bottle in the bottom of the boat where someone might just trip over it.

If there are no squid, you might be lucky, as I was, to pass the time watching a pod of pothead whales, or spot two bald eagles take flight from their perches on the sheer bluffs which rear up from the water line.

For more than 10 years, Eugene was forced to leave home after the summer fishing season to find work on freighters out of Nova Scotian ports. It is a pattern Burin men have been repeating for longer than most care to remember. In 1950, more than half of the work force of the Burin Peninsula was away from home for most of the year, either employed at the U.S. air force and naval bases in St. John's and Argentia, or, like Eugene, shipping out of mainland harbours.

Eugene is one of an expatriated generation of "Petit Forte Boys" who has returned to claim his birthright.

"Well, boy, I been on the boats all these winters, and all I saw was hard work. And you were always working for somebody else. I found after going around as much as I did that I was just as well off or better in Petit Forte as I would be anywhere else, so I built this house, got married and stayed here ever since."

Eugene built a modern bungalow for his bride, and, like many outport couples, the Joneses moved in on their wedding night. There are six new bungalows under construction. Architecturally bland — the ubiquitous Canadian house — they are nevertheless important symbols of a brighter future for Petit Forte, which teetered on the brink of extinction for a decade.

Eugene remembers when he left home in 1969: " First when I left it didn't look very good, because resettling was on then. It went down to 17 households and it looked for a while that they were going to go too."

In its initial form, the programme required, as a precondition for government assistance, that the whole community agree to resettle. Many must have felt that they had no choice, for those who held out did so at the risk of angering their neighbours. It made "bad friends."

13

The incentive was hard cash, more than most outport Newfoundlanders had ever had in their pockets before: a basic $1,000 grant plus $200 for each member of the family up to a maximum of $3,200. It proved, however, to be barely adequate to begin a new life in the growth centres.

"There are people who made it better, quite a few," admits Eugene Jones, adding quickly, "there were an awful lot of people who made it worse, too." Many discovered to their dismay that they had to return to their old homes in the summer to make ends meet. "They know nothing, only fish. What are they going to do in St. John's? Nothing," was the way one Petit Forte fisherman summed up the predicament of many who resettled.

Earl and Bride Hickey have been coming back to Petit Forte every summer since they resettled in the late 1960s in Southern Harbour, a town with a population of 759, which received people from Bar Haven, Davis Cove, Red Island, Port Royal, St. Anne's, St. Joseph's and Gladys Harbour, all outports from the Placentia Bay area. At 71, Earl still fishes, though more to please himself, and he cuts his own firewood. He's quick to point out that he can't do either in Southern Harbour.

"I never earned a dollar since I got down there. We didn't really realize what we were up against until we got there. They were saying the coastal boat was going to be taken. They were going to take the school, we'd be left with nothing. They were more or less drivin' you out. Now it's better than it ever was."

In the late 1960s, the community's morale reached a low point. Those who stayed were unsure whether they would be able to hold out much longer. The houses and stages began to show signs of needing maintenance. By the early 1970s, however, those who had persevered began to feel that their instincts had been correct. They could see what was happening to those who had left.

Then, in 1974, the Smallwood government was overturned, and the growth centre concept was phased out in favour of a grass-roots approach to rural development. Small communities throughout the province organized and incorporated as regional development associations. They now determine their own needs, then lobby government. The government provides funds for the hiring of a full-time co-ordinator for each association and sponsors leadership training courses. "We're offering self-help," says George Green of the Department of Rural, Agricultural and Northern Development.

Petit Forte was a charter member of the Placentia West Development Association, which now represents 10 communities.

Eric Hayden is vice-president. Two years ago, at age 39, he dissolved his successful survey business in Labrador City and returned to the ancestral place, Hayden's Point, to fish.

Eric is rediscovering the private comforts of a small place— "Here I have no bad friends"— and he emphasizes that the community projects often entail a personal sacrifice: "I know in a lot of instances people went to work here and lost money, as they could stay home and draw fairly good unemployment. But they went to work because they knew what they were doing was for the good of the community."

The past few winters, for Canada Works' minimum wage, the men have upgraded the fish storage facility, built a new government wharf, and last year erected the community's pride, a medical clinic, which is visited biweekly by a doctor who helicopters in from Come-by-Chance.

There are 30 households and 120 full time residents in Petit Forte today, half as many as before resettlement, but the number is growing modestly every year. Another nearby outport, South East Bight, like Petit Forte, hung on through resettlement, and is now undergoing a revival. And a handful of families are once again overwintering just across the sound in neighbouring Little Paradise, which, in fact, did resettle.

All three communities now belong to the Placentia West Association. President Henry Moores of Rushoon says, "Every community is behind each other. That makes everything fall in place. I don't know, boy, it's almost too good to be true."

The renaissance that Petit Forte has experienced to date has gone hand in hand with a remarkable upswing in the inshore fishery, which itself was occasioned by Canada's declaration of a 200-mile fishing limit. Nevertheless, Neil Murray, editor of *The Union Forum,* the house organ of the Newfoundland Fishermen, Food and Allied Workers Union, warns, "The Union has found that a lot was false expectation. There are still a limited number of people who can make a living." In fact, the Union's position is that the present number of people in the fishery cannot be sustained without government price support, and, at the Union's urging, there are currently tight restrictions in place on the issuing of new licences. That worries Eugene Jones: "That's one of the things that's

15

going to make it bad for these places, if a young fellow comes out of school and can't get a licence. If he's gotta go and find a job, you don't know if he's going to come back or what he's going to do."

The inshore fisherman's average net income is $8,000 to $9,000 for a season that extends from April to October. During the off-season he is eligible to collect unemployment insurance. It seems little enough, but a man's standard of living in an outport like Petit Forte is higher than the raw figures would indicate. It must be remembered that he does not have car expenses nor, in most cases, a mortgage. He hunts, fishes and cuts his own firewood. He is a self-styled carpenter, plumber and electrician, and if the job requires more than two hands, the neighbours can be counted upon. There's not a young couple here that doesn't have a few thousand in the bank.

"The Road" is a footpath, really, that at its widest can accommodate three men abreast — if they don't swing their arms. It circles "The Harbour" between the stages and the houses, beginning at Hayden's Point and petering out, a mile away, among the rocks. I found that I never reached my destination without first stopping for a yarn with those I met.

The Road's one sidebranch ambles up Church Hill and along Jones Cove. Just past the church, a new punt, its hull half planked in, rests its keel in a yard. It is Mike Lake's first effort as a boat builder and he admits to being heartened by the approving nods —no more — of the old-timers.

Mike grew up in Rushoon, a nearby resettlement centre which now boasts a population of 700. His father fished, but there is little fishing done there now. Most of the young men settle for seasonal work on "The Track," laying rail line for the Canadian Pacific Railway in western Canada. They stay long enough to collect unemployment insurance, then return home for the winter.

Next year, he hopes to launch his 25-foot boat and, where it now rests, to build a new home for his family: his wife Evelyn, a native of Petit Forte, and their infant son, Michael.

"First time I came down here, I was talking to people same as if I knew them a long time," Mike remembers. "This is home to me now. I wouldn't move."

In Petit Forte, people are proud that their doors are left unlocked — "You goes out to someone's house and no knocking, you walk in. Here we find it strange for someone to knock on the door. You think, Is someone dead or what?"

Doors open into kitchens. Most are appointed with two stoves, a woodburning Enterprise or Fawcett and an electric range. You can see your face reflected in their chrome. And in the women's eyes, grandmother and girlchild alike, a clarity shines out, as if the order of their home was a reflection of some inner sanctuary.

Monday: Bread is rising on the warming oven. Through the window I can see rows of wash flapping in the sea breeze. A crucifix hangs on the lintel. The icons of Catholicism have their station in each Petit Forte home as surely as do family portraits. If it is an old house like this one, there is a day bed next to a window, the exposed ceiling beams are generously coated with white gloss paint. I accept the customary offer of a drink.

"I didn't want to come home," recalls Maureen Pearson. "I more or less figured that we'd get back in Petit Forte and I'd be stuck in the house all the time with nothing to do." Maureen is now post mistress.

The children, too, have adjusted to outport life. "The children love it here," their mother says. "It's not like in Labrador City where we lived on a busy street. Now they have their breakfast and they're gone, and you don't worry about them."

"The children are some keen now," their grandmother chimes in. "But if they grow up here, they know the simpler things too."

The simpler things: climbing the hills which, to a child, must seem of mythic proportions; trout fishing or handlining for tomcods and cunners which cruise around every wharf where they eagerly devour whatever offal is thrown their way; or taking a Sunday boat ride with the family to Port Anne or Paradise, where someone is sure to get out an accordion or harmonica.

Aubrey Pearson had a well-paying job as a millwright in Labrador City when he and Maureen came back to Petit Forte in the spring of 1978 to wait out the strike. They put their house in Labrador City on the market, not expecting it to sell. When it did, they decided to stay in Petit Forte, an option that had not been open to either of them as teenagers.

Aubrey left home in 1965 to work on a freighter: "Joey (Smallwood) was on the go. You haul up your boats and burn them. There was going to be no more fishery. At the same time, there wasn't too much future here."

17

Maureen did what most girls of her generation were obliged to do, leave home to finish high school. (Many still do, although the two teachers in Petit Forte are qualified to graduate high school students.) Maureen believes times have changed for the better: "In Lab City, Aubrey was making a lot more money than we do here but I find we can save more and get whatever we want in Petit Forte. Most of the young people who are growing up now, they're not going to be leaving, they'll stay here."

If they do there may once again be houses on "The Other Side," as the shore opposite the harbour is known. As at Darby's Harbour, a clearing at the water's edge is the only sign that people once lived there.

"That would be nice," Maureen says, with a longing in her voice, "to look over at night and see the lights again."

The light source wouldn't be kerosene, as it was before resettlement. Five years ago, electricity came to Petit Forte, supplied by three 180-horse power generators. Two years ago, telephones were installed. "We got a little slice of everything that was going," says Eugene Jones, who credits the Development Association.

The chief object of conjecture these days is the road that would connect Petit Forte to the rest of the island. It would have to penetrate 15 miles of dauntingly rugged terrain.

The CN coastal boat, *Hopedale*, pulled out of Petit Forte at 5:00 a.m. under cover of heavy fog.

There was freight aboard to be unloaded in Monkstown. As I looked, with the same awe-struck humility, at the shoreline I had passed just a few days earlier with Billie Synard, I thought of what his wife said to me of their resettlement from Port Elizabeth on Flat Island to Baine Harbour: "The place you're born, you can't forget."

During the 1950's and 1960's, when resettlement was taking place in Newfoundland, a whole generation of Canadians were, similarly, being deracinated by the trends in society which made people more mobile — and that mobility one-directional, toward the cities and towns. In Newfoundland, the phenomenon was more remarkable because the government showed its hand — often a heavy one.

Whether in Newfoundland or elsewhere in Canada, the essence of the small place was community spirit. It existed, quite simply, because people needed each other. Nowhere, perhaps, has this been more evident than in outport Newfoundland. The environment demanded that people stick together, to maintain a hold on that narrow place which the sea and land had surrendered to them. It wasn't only a matter of surviving the elements, however. You made your own fun too, you celebrated together. They still do in Petit Forte, whether by seeing the sun up at a wedding party or just dropping in for "a little argument, a few cards and a drink."

In Petit Forte, the extended family is alive and well; there's a genuine neighbourliness, a graciousness toward strangers and a rugged individualism which needs the presence of others to define itself. For those of us who left such a place, it is a vital example of what we thought only existed in memory, and it approaches the ideal sought by the counter-culture generation that fled the cities.

None of the talk of resettlement prepared me for the desolation of Big Paradise, once a vibrant neighbour to Petit Forte. There, as had occurred on my entry into Petit Forte harbour, the first thing to catch my attention was the church. The steeple of the Big Paradise church is red also, but there all similarity ends. You see that the roof is collapsed, that the rafters only support the low ceiling of an impassive sky. The gay colours that were once someone's fancy are fading from the walls. Soon the houses will be the colour of the winter sea, the colour of rock. They sit mouldering, abject, at land's end.

Little Paradise is separated from its counterpart by a rocky point. We made anchor in the deep harbour, while a motorboat came out to meet us with passengers bound for Argentia. Some people return here in the summer to fish. And the last few years, a handful of families have overwintered. I recall Maureen Pearson's simple history of Petit Forte and its own recovery from Smallwood's resettlement: "A few people, they were stubborn, they wouldn't leave because their friends were staying or their family.... Now there's people coming back." She is right, and I now understand the proud, stubborn gleam that came into her eye as she said it.

END OF THE TRAIL

This is a forgotten shore and that's a shame. For nowhere in Nova Scotia will you pass through white clapboard villages with a better prospect of the sea than along the Chignecto peninsula, north of Parrsboro. With the great blue bulk of the Minas Basin stretched out by your side, the road dips, climbs and switchbacks through lonely vistas of hardwood which clothe the Cobequid Mountains. Through V-shaped mountain slots, you can sight Cape Split and Cape Blomidon, headlands worthy of their place in Micmac tradition as the seats of power of the man-god Glooscap. The sheer basalt of Cape Split rises defiantly from the water line to its 122-meter anvil-top, overlooking the whirlpools and torturous currents of the Minas Channel which foam with the fury of the Bay of Fundy's comings-and-goings.

It never ceases to surprise me that so few Nova Scotians are familiar with this 32-kilometre stretch of shoreline, known as the Parrsboro Shore. Residents proudly call it "The Little Cabot Trail." Chauvinism aside, it is well-named, for it offers up the most spectacular Nova Scotian seascape west of Cheticamp.

The village of Advocate Harbour stands at the end of this yet-to-be-discovered tourist route. It is flanked by two mountainous headlands of its own, Cape d'Or and Cape Chignecto — cradling the sister communities of East and West Advocate — and faces the eminence of Isle Haute. The houses of the three communities, locally called Advocate for short, form a continuous string like colonies of white barnacles hugging the shoreline. The dramatic setting impresses with an almost unearthly quality as if it had been laid out on the easel of a 19th century romantic landscape painter.

The harbour is protected at its mouth by a natural breakwater of driftwood that has piled up along a 6-km-long sandbar. The narrow difficult entrance to this snug berth was well known to the coastal trade. Also, Advocate men followed the sea in locally built ships with names as exotic as their destinations — like *Calcutta* and *Amazon*.

According to the historian Frederick J. Pohl, Advocate Harbour was the stopping place of Prince Henry Sinclair, the Earl of Orkney, 100 years before Columbus's voyage of discovery. Pohl makes a convincing case for the Earl's New World explorations, and believes Sinclair built a new ship in Advocate Harbour in 1398 to return to the Orkneys.

There are clear and indisputable records of Samuel de Champlain's exploits here in the 17th century. He came to Advocate Harbour, which he called Port of Mines (the name later given to the greater Basin), in search of copper. With a navigator's keen eye, he described his cautious introduction to the harbour: "To enter one must lay down buoys, and mark a sandbar which lies at the entrance, and runs along a channel parallel with the opposite coast of the mainland. Then one enters a bay about a league in length and half a league in width. In some places the bottom is muddy and sandy, and vessels can there lie aground. The tide falls from four to five fathoms."

Today there are a half-dozen fishing boats beached by the side of the wharf, waiting to be refloated by the tide. For now, the famous Fundy tide has retreated, turning the harbour into a muddy lagoon.

The fortunes of the town also seem to be on an ebb. People here have always depended on the fishery and the forests but these once bountiful resources have been severely depleted in recent years. Local fishermen claim that the fishing's been bad ever since Polish factory ships anchored off Cape d'Or several years ago and scooped up the spawning herring stocks. Now, many residents fear that Scott Paper's 30-year onslaught on the Cape Chignecto timber stands is reaching its inevitable conclusion. Some people in town say that the next decade could see the community's largest employer pull out. And all the talk about tourist potential is just that: talk and potential.

Advocate is facing up to these grim prospects in what seems an unusual, even novel, way in these times of increasing dependence on government initiative. They have formed a good old-fashioned self-help group. The Advocate and District Action Organization got its start in 1979 when a local farmer's barn burned down. Bernard

Elliot was in his early 60's, had no insurance and, it looked to him, no option but to abandon farming.

Byron Hefferon, the United Church minister at the time, called a community meeting to deal with Elliot's plight and eventually his neighbours raised $2500. Scott Paper donated free stumpage; volunteers cut, trucked and sawed the logs. The new barn went up in a week. It was the first barn building bee in the community's living memory, and people frankly surprised themselves with what they had accomplished. In fact, the notion of community self-help looked too good to just let it drop.

Since then, the Action Organization has replaced a home for a family that was burned out and met other day-to-day emergencies, by supplying milk and home heating fuel to families whose unemployment insurance had been cut off.

Walton Rector, a retired car salesman, was the first president of the group and is now the area's county councillor. He's seen the changes in attitude that the self-help model produced: "A lot of young people gained confidence and have come to realize that you can do something if you are willing to co-operate and work together."

Co-operation is one thing, tackling the economic ills that afflict the community as a whole quite another proposition. However, the action group has begun to turn its attention to community works—in effect , to act as a village council—and recently it undertook its most ambitious project, the construction of a recreation complex to meet current local and projected tourist needs.

They have laid out a ball field, replete with bleachers, dugouts and an outfield fence, the latter scrounged from a derelict outdoor hockey rink. Tying the project together will be a log recreation centre, which is being funded by a government grant. Rector insists, however, that it is not just another make-work project with no hope of paying returns on the taxpayer's investment. He sees a cottage craft industry in the recreation centre's basement, and eventually, log cabins and a motel for tourists, a camping area, and perhaps even a tennis court in the old gravel pit.

"That's my vision," Rector says, casting his eyes over the now idle acres at the back of the village. "It's reasonable, and let's say, I have high hopes."

Rector pauses, then adds in an exasperated tone: "That god-damned road is the whole key."

22

That road is now a broken line on the province's highway map; in reality, a dirt track that connects Advocate to Joggins, Nova Scotia and completes the loop around the Chignecto peninsula. Advocate stands at the apex of the triangular peninsula where it juts into the Bay of Fundy like the prow of a ship. Rector maintains that tourists avoid the unpaved section "because they don't like gravel roads and they don't like backtracking." As a consequence, most never reach Advocate to see what it has to offer: Fishing, hunting, beachcombing, but mostly, magnificent solitude.

Rector doesn't want handouts, just incentive to allow the area to be its own ambassador: "I feel that if the highway is opened up, tourism will gradually develop on its own through the private sector."

However, the Action Organization's perennial petitioning of government to pave the road so far hasn't paid off. It is not so surprising, for the area is a political barren. With the exception of New Salem and Apple River, there are only lumbering ghost towns between Advocate and Joggins.

Local tourism boosters argue, perhaps rightly, that the backwoods ambience is just the tonic the Trans-Canada and city-weary traveller is seeking. There is an irony at the heart of this virtue, however, for the area's unsullied beauty is the last natural resource with which people can bargain with the outside world.

Burnell Reid is 70. Like his father before him he operated a sawmill. He remembers when he could hear the whistles of three other locally owned mills every morning. In 1967 his own became the last to close. Now there is only a pile of rotting sawdust to mark where it sat on the beach at West Advocate, and a colour snapshot in his kitchen to remind him of what it looked like.

Reid saw the writing on the wall. He was not going to be able to compete, either for the best woodsmen or access to the best timber, with Scott Paper Maritimes Ltd., which had established a large sawmill in Parrsboro. "So," he recalls with resignation, "we got out before we had to get out."

The closing of Reid's mill also signalled the passing of a time-honoured approach to forest management. Reid was of a generation of local lumbermen who would not cut a tree that was less than a foot in diameter at the butt. It was a practise that ensured a wood supply for the future. "But when the big companies came in and when they put a road through, they wanted everything cut that was there," Reid explains, "because they could move out of here and not come back for 100 years."

Reid's speculation has the unsettling ring of prophecy. In recent years, Scott has mounted a reforestation program, but Reid is not alone in thinking it may be too little too late.

"A few years ago, before they came in on this clear cut, they said they were going to farm our woods, replant and farm, and that our woods were all going to come back. They were going to show *us* how to produce lumber.

"But before they got done— just go and take a picture. The destruction! There'll be no more cutting for maybe 125 or 150 years," Reid insists.

To make matters worse, the reforestation program itself runs contrary to Reid's lifetime experience of the Acadian forest: "One thing the people resent the most of anything is this replanting and then spraying to kill off all the hardwood. It's natural for our forests to have spruce and hardwood. And if you change the thing, it's not going to work.

"Oh, it might work for one generation," Reid concedes, "but then the land's going to run out."

With the timber resource promising a slow recovery at best, and the fishery in apparent decline, what does it augur for Advocate's future? "It's a good place for retirement, old age pensioners, and that's what we're going to have the most of," Reid says sadly.

Still, there are young people willing to stake their future in Advocate.

One of them is Gerry Field. "I was one of the first to break the chain of young guys leaving." After finishing high school, Gerry cut pulp for Scott Paper, which is often the only employment option open to the community's young men. He found that the work not only jarred his bones but rankled his principles, too. "I helped them slaughter the land," he says with regret. "If it wasn't for the need of money, I wouldn't have done it."

For the past two years, he's turned his back to the woods and looked to the sea for a living. At the same time, he erected a 9-meter tower that commands a view of the tide-rip off Cape d'Or, and the blue finger of land on the horizon that is the Annapolis Valley's North Mountain range. The tower, his self-built home and the acre of garden that surround both stand as stubborn symbols of Field's new-found independence, his determination to make subsistence farming and part-time fishing a way of life, much as Advocate's early settlers did.

The fishing, however, hasn't been as good as he would like. "It used to be," he says, with the air of an old salt, "you could fill a boat off there, but now you don't know whether you'll get enough for a meal."

Like most fishermen, Field is always hopeful. His optimism that the fish will return is shared by Mike Fraser. The two young men plan to fish together this summer.

Fraser, 19, could be found this spring in a boatshop that belongs to his granduncle, Captain William Morris, at 80 one of the last of a generation of Advocate men to distinguish themselves as sea captains. While Fraser worked feverishly, fitting his Cape Islander with a new keel and replacing worn out planking, Captain Morris watched admiringly: "I couldn't do that at his age — I couldn't do that now."

Fraser doesn't have illusions about the standard of living that fishing can provide. He says that he'll be happy if he can net $10,000. Although there's always risk associated with making a living from the sea — particularly, given the area's precarious stocks — it's as reliable, perhaps more so, than work in the woods.

"There's never been steady work here. You never know whether it's going to snow and you'd be 13 or 14 stamps short. Then you'd have no money all winter," Fraser explains.

This uncertainty has bred a deep-rooted fatalism in many young people. "Pogey" is as much an accepted way of life in Advocate as it is in other small, isolated Maritime towns where the work is seasonal. The recent nine-month Abercrombie plant strike against Scott Paper shut down the woods and removed even that economic crutch. It provided a disturbing glimpse into what might be in store for the community if Scott Paper ever did pack its bags: Idleness and tension spilled out in acts of vandalism. "What is there for young guys to do but drink and raise hell?" rationalized one disenchanted youth.

Jet Robinson's General Store was a target of the discontent. "It gives a guy a funny feeling to come in and find the window blown out like that," Robinson says, pointing to his office window which bears the unmistakable pattern of a shotgun blast.

"You go home at night and see the tide coming and going, and you think it's such a peaceful place; then you have ridiculous things like that happen."

Robinson, who left a dairy farm in Connecticut and followed a "Land for Sale" ad in *Field & Stream* to Advocate, is philosophical about what could easily be interpreted as local bigotry. He points out that he hasn't been the only victim, and that business has actually picked up since the incidents started.

"I was rather impressed with how well we were received by the town, and especially after we took over the store. Small town people — I think they're a warmer type of person."

The doctor comes in and Robinson promptly plunks a fresh halibut down on the counter: "This is for you." Someone, wishing to remain anonymous, has left it as a gift, in the tradition of small town gratitude for a service.

That same week, Dr. Maurice Meyers was planning to leave his post as the only doctor at the rambling farmhouse that has served as the community hospital since 1945. Advocate's relative isolation makes having its own hospital a necessity, especially to cope with woods accidents and obstetrical emergencies. Older patients like it because it's homier, but the staff has to adjust to antiquated equipment, such as the 40-year-old U.S. Army field unit x-ray which, Meyers points out, is identical to the model Klinger used on *M*A*S*H*. "A fellow straight out of medical school would have quite a problem," he says.

Meyer, who served in Canada's North, was attracted by the professional and personal independence that Advocate's rustic isolation offered. However, after four years, he began to recognize the creeping signs of rural doctor burnout: "In the old days," he reflects, "you had somebody to drive your horse, now you have to drive yourself." Meyers was the 14th doctor to serve Advocate in the last 30 years. He plans on semi-retirement, but will return to the area to spend time at his cottage.

The area seems to hold a special attraction for individualists like Meyers. Notable among them was playwright and actor Sam Shepherd. Shepherd was a 1960s cohort of Allen Ginsberg and Bob Dylan, but gained a modicum of academic respectability by copping the coveted Pulitzer Prize for drama in 1979 for his play *Buried Child*. "Sam was deep," remembers a neighbour.

Shepherd hasn't been back to Advocate in two decades. While living there he owned the house that once belonged to Captain Joshua Dewis. Dewis was the builder of what just might be the world's most famous sailing ship, the *Marie Celeste*. Christened the *Amazon,* she was launched in neighbouring Spencer's Island in 1861. In 1872, the ship was found abandoned in the mid-Atlantic. The crew's food was on the table, but no trace of them was ever found. Their fate remains a mystery to this day.

Joshua's grandson, Rhodes Dewis, still lives in Advocate. He remembers his grandfather's common sense version of events. The *Mary Celeste* was carrying a cargo of alcohol. Spontaneous combustion took place, blowing the hatch off: " He said all that happened was they panicked. They jumped ship and didn't attach a line, and the ship drifted away from them — they just made a stupid move."

Dewis is now in his 70s. As a boy he remembers playing in what is now his grassy beachside yard, among the ribs of vessels shaped by the hands of some of the world's best shipwrights. Between 1820 and 1920 nearly 700 wooden ships were built and launched from the Parrsboro shore. During that era, Advocate was neither isolated nor inward-looking but almost cosmopolitan, and as evidence Dewis produces from the parlour a ceramic jam jar that his grandmother brought back from a trip to Bombay in 1882. He fears that such proud ancestral memories will be lost with his generation: "It's only the last few years that people have been writing the history down."

Don Gamblin, a young teacher at the Advocate District School, has been doing his part to keep alive memories of Advocate's more halcyon days, when it boasted a furrier, photography salon and several hotels. He's been getting his social studies class to assemble a scrapbook of old photographs. They show a prosperous sawmill in the ghost town of Eatonville, mining row houses at the abandoned Cape d'Or copper mine, sailing ships in Advocate Harbour, decks piled high with deal. In every photograph, proud men — in some cases, the children's grandfathers — stand before the camera sure of their small but important place in history.

"Some ask, 'What happened?'"

Gamblin recounts the familiar story of the demise of wooden ships that ravaged local economies. However, he still sees the resourcefulness in the Advocate people that accounted for their entrepreneurial past.

"People from this area have their own unique character," Gamblin maintains. "If you look at the people in this area and their ability to do things on their own, they have a lot of natural resources to draw on. I learn from them all the time. If I want to fix something or, say, build a patio deck, I don't buy a book; I go and ask one of my buddies."

This innate resourcefulness has helped residents survive the bad times. The recession of the early 1980s forced many young people to return to the area. As one young man, who had spent a few years in Alberta, told me: "You can pick up odd jobs — nobody starves around here." At least in Advocate they have the support of family, and, as recent history has shown, of the community if circumstances warrant it.

Action Organization President, Arthur Fillmore, spent 15 years in the services before moving back home. He believes, "If the economy stays the way it is, I think people are better off in a community like this one rather than in a larger town or city."

However, Fillmore acknowledges that there is little future if the tourist potential isn't developed to offset the loss of jobs in the forest and fishery. He's confident that it can be: "I've been over the Cabot Trail, and I think it's every bit as pretty here. It's just not as long, that's all."

Right now, many tourists who come to Advocate get there quite by accident by taking a wrong turn at Parrsboro. "Once they are here," says William Morris, proprietor of the Harbour Lite restaurant, "they can't understand why there are so few people around."

II. THE STRUGGLE

I grew up on a small farm, and as I say in "The Fat Of The Land," we made do in a mixed way. Even so, as a child I had the distinct impression that we were rich; my mother recalls with humour that I said as much. True, we were not rich judging by today's inflated standards. But the land provided for our basic needs (the food was fresh, organically grown, tasty), and I think my illusion was closer to reality than might first appear to be the case. The lifestyle of the family farm was enriching in a spiritual sense, and I felt this wholeness as one feels the warmth of a March sun.

Leaving the farm was a shock that created 'a longing in me all my life' — to return to the land. I did eventually, though as a writer, not a farmer like my father. Making a living on the land has become increasingly difficult in the thirty years since our farm failed. Doing so requires huge capital investment, destructive agricultural practices and an unquestioning commitment to the agribusiness system. A few farmers cling to the notion of mixed farming; some even continue to farm the way my father did, separating cream for butter-making. I rediscovered a part of myself in looking at their way of life and farming — which, not so long ago, were one and the same thing.

But the struggle to keep the land in production is daunting. In the decade since "The Fat Of The Land" first appeared, the number of cream shippers has declined by two-thirds, to fewer than 100. That compares with 8,000 when our farm was sold and went out of production in 1960.

Urban sprawl puts unrelenting pressure on productive land, and increasing numbers of urban dwellers are escaping the city in search of a patch of unsullied nature. Hundreds of thousands of such people visit Prince Edward Island every year. However, a few have not been content to leave the island with memories of its pastoral charm; they have wanted to acquire a chunk of the island for themselves, and furthermore, to exclude local people from common areas — in effect to set aside their own fiefdom as did the Island's 18th-century, absentee landlords. The struggle for control of the Greenwich dune on P.E.I. (detailed in "Storming The Sand Castles") epitomizes this battle between traditional use of the land and development exclusively for the sake of outsiders' pleasure.

What the ongoing Greenwich controversy underscores is the deep commitment Islanders have to the land. For many it is not simply another commodity to be bought and sold, but something history has imbued with personal values and therefore must be protected and respected in much the same way as a family heirloom.

ELEMENTS OF BEGINNING

I wanted to look out from a rise of land, to look *over* the land, and on spring nights when the bedroom curtain lifted on a breeze, to hear the voice of water in the darkness, speaking its secrets of speckled trout. Eight years ago, when I bought the place I now call home, I was acting on an urge to return to the environment of my childhood — of hill, brook, and saltwater — which had created a longing in me all my life.

The place where I grew up was called Brook Farm. Its namesake rose at the back of my father's 100 acres and descended through spruce and alder to empty into the tidal Chebogue River at the southwestern tip of Nova Scotia. The West Brook (which gives my new community its name) rises in the Cobequid Hills, connects with the Maccan River, which wends between 300-year-old Acadian dykes to join the great tides of the Bay of Fundy in northern Nova Scotia.

Nova Scotia is surrounded by a bay, a gulf and an ocean. The peninsular province hangs onto Canada by the hinge of the Tantramar Marsh — hangs there like an old door on a windowless house. On Dad's saltwater farm, with its tides and herons, April gifts of smelt and sea trout, its minnows and marshpools, I was constantly aware of the ocean's influence. But even here, ten minutes from the sea and circled by hardwood hills, in December I can lean over our bridge and through a pane of new ice, spy salmon, still silver from the salt water, waiting to mix their seed in the gravel of our summer swimming hole.

Nova Scotians are a bit like those salmon, irresistibly drawn to the sea and irresistibly drawn back to their birthplace, as if by some biological imperative. There are really only two kinds of Nova Scotians: those who leave and long to come home (many eventually do) and those who can never bring themselves to leave. I am one of the latter.

Two generations ago, "the Bluenosers" who left crossed the Gulf of Maine to the "the Boston States," as Nova Scotians like to call New England. Many prospered, it seems. Tokens of their newfound affluence arrived in what we called "The Boston Barrel," care packages of hand-me-downs and church basement bargains. A generation ago, the emigration was "down the road" to Ontario. In my generation, the flow temporarily reversed itself, as long-haired American youth bought up marginal land. Over the next decade, many trickled home, having become disillusioned with the romance of the past. Stubbornly, Nova Scotians cling to the past, but it is the one of history not of dreams.

As fate would have it, I live in a 160-year-old house, which, like the one at Brook Farm, is the oldest in the community. Its unshakeable post-and- beam frame stands proudly overlooking thirty acres, more or less. I never considered myself a back-to-the-lander. I lacked the idealism, having seen my father's farm fail like so many others. But I care for the land enough to use it as best I can.

A neighbour takes the hay off our five-acres of cleared land. The garden fills our freezer. The sidehill of wild blueberries stands ready to yield a commercial crop or carboys of homemade wine. (In winter it provides an exhilarating toboggan or cross-country ski run.) In March the 75-year-old sugar maples give jars of amber syrup, in August, ample shade. By Victoria Day in May — when in theory it's warm enough to go skinny-dipping in Nova Scotia — the fiddleheads will be unfurling along the brook; a month later, I can take my daughter down the hill to catch a meal of trout. In July, a perennial miracle transpires: Thimble-size strawberries appear in the hay field, an organic legacy of the farmer who prudently left off cultivating this hillside, a generation ago.

I now realize that there was something instinctive about my choice of this place on the hill. A physical homing principle was at work, as in the salmon when it detects in the salt universe of the sea that first fresh molecule of its native brook, the elements of its beginnings guiding it home.

THE FAT OF THE LAND

The last of our calves that I remember was born weak. It was not the first time that it had happened. The barn was all but empty, our herd reduced to two cows from the usual complement of eight. The calf had not been tongued dry by its mother when I first saw it. I kept vigil with my mother, sharing her anxiety and sense of helplessness, during the first few days of the newborn's life. The calf did not survive. All the stanchions were soon idle, the rituals of separating the cream and churning the butter were things of the past. My brothers and I argued over who would mix the packet of food colouring into the ghastly vegetable lard which replaced our homemade butter at the table.

Bang's disease, the cause of the abortions and weak calf syndrome, dealt the final blow to the farm. But the move was inevitable. For 20 years the farm had provided a meagre income — never enough for a new coat of house paint, but always enough to keep us warmly clothed and well fed. Milk, butter, eggs, vegetables and pork for the table came from the farm. We sold surplus from our market garden locally, cut pulp, exported a few crates of blueberries on the Boston boat, and, in later years, my father worked part-time as a carpenter in town. In short, we made do in a mixed way. Always, however, the mainstay was the cream cheque. Without it the farm had no future. It was 1960.

In 1960, 8,000 cream shipping farms were scattered from Cape Breton Island to the southern tip of Nova Scotia, where I grew up. Today, there are fewer than 300. Most of these are concentrated along the North Shore of Nova Scotia, in proximity to the three creameries which still accept farm-separated cream for the manufacture of butter. There were once 27. Located in small towns and villages, the creameries were an integral part of the local economies. Why cream producing farms have been ravaged numerically and, in some circles, held up to ridicule, has as much to do with social changes external to the farm as on-the-farm common sense.

In 1967, a Milk Industry Inquiry concluded that three-quarters of all dairy farms in Nova Scotia were "uneconomic units." Although the Inquiry Committee stopped short of recommending that the small shipper (of cream and milk) be legislated out of existence, effectively, he was being asked to hang it up or be squeezed out. It was proposed that cream shippers undertake the capital intensive transition to whole milk production, or withdraw.

Between 1963 and 1967, more than 3,000 cream producers had gone out of production and the verdict of "The Inquiry," as it is still known, seemed to place the capstone on a dying industry. It predicted a future for the cream producers that was discouraging at best, with "pressure resulting from land consolidation, increased costs of production and increased costs of pickup and transportation" all working against the small dairymen.

The cream producer separates his own milk on the farm, selling the cream for butter production and retaining the skim milk for conversion into a product for which there is a demand: pork, veal or poultry. Cream producers believe that they should occupy a special niche in the dairy industry and that there are convincing arguments for the preservation of their place in an increasingly hostile bureaucracy.

The decline in their numbers, in fact, has abated in recent years. There has been an infusion of new blood. This so-called "new wave" of cream shippers has revived the defunct Cream Producers' Association. The biggest challenge facing them is to convince the government that they are not an anachronism.

The perception of the cream producer as someone who is less than a professional dairyman persists. The stereotype: a man over 50 who milks a few cows in summer when they are on pasture. In winter he dries the herd off. He may, but just as likely not, feed the skim milk to hogs or veal calves. His greatest asset is the land he sits on. It is paid off, and when he tires of farming, he will sell it for non-agricultural purposes and have a tidy nest egg for retirement. In the eyes of government he is apathetic and inefficient, a hobbyist who farms as a lifestyle, not a business.

That the image is not without example does little to convince the government that they should provide incentive to the cream

34

sector. For the new wave of cream shippers, it makes their way all the more uphill struggle.

One of the new wave is David Butlin. He and his wife, Nina, arrived in Nova Scotia in 1975. For several years, they had homesteaded in partnership with six other couples on 280 acres, near Hundred Mile House, B.C. "It was difficult for us," Nina recalls. "We wanted to farm and it wasn't the ideal place to be farming. We would have required as much capital to clear land as to buy a farm." Then, David came across a fateful article about cream shippers in Nova Scotia. "We had the idea that here was a market we could hit," says David, "and we were interested in dairy."

The Butlins came to Nova Scotia with other convictions: They wanted cleared, arable land with a house on it; they didn't want to clear or to build again. And, if they were going to live in Nova Scotia, they wanted to be near the water. After a nine-month tour of the province, they settled on Tatamagouche. It was not only on the Northumberland Strait, it had a creamery. "Things began to gel."

One day in December, when the first winter storm was blowing itself out, I decided to walk the long unploughed driveway to Crackwillow Farm. It had been a year since I last visited the Butlins. Nina was in the kitchen. Stainless steel buckets of tallow were rendering slowly on the blacktop furthest from the firebox. I found David in the basement at the cutting table, where a side of beef was in stages of becoming hamburger, roasts and steaks. The other half of the cull cow was hanging in the cool air.

At supper, David was justifiably proud of the good taste of his organically raised Guernsey beef. To top things off, there was heavy, golden cream for the coffee. It was fare that I was to share in every household, while making my rounds in pursuit of the economics and lifestyle of cream shipping: home-raised meat and heavy cream which makes money in your cup, if not always for the farm ledger.

The Butlins' is still known locally as the "Willie Arthur place." David and Nina valued local opinion in making their choice of a farm. "People told us that Willie Arthur raised a cracking fine family off that place. It was renowned. If any place should produce, it should be this place, we thought." David's laugh is tinged with irony.

On arrival in Nova Scotia, they also sought out advice at the Nova Scotia Agricultural College on what kind of farming they were recommending. The flat answer was nothing. "I imagine the answer is still nothing," says Nina. "To me that's the wrong answer."

David goes on: "There doesn't seem to be enough attention paid to givens in farming, to climate, soil, and the type of land that you have and what it is capable of producing. If you look at these factors and limit yourself to the type of farming that is suited to what you're given, then you don't come up with trying to grow corn in Nova Scotia. You come up with a forage-based farming. Cream shipping fits the bill."

The Butlins were undeterred by the chilling negativity of the experts' answer. They had to wait a year before there was quota available, but with one cow (aptly named Butterscotch), a milk pail and less than $10,000 up front, they started producing. "It's an opportunity that is rare in Canada and in Nova Scotia," says Nina."I don't think that it's appreciated how rare it is."

The stakes were soon raised by what David calls the animal inflation factor. As the return per animal decreases due to inflation, more animals must be acquired to make ends meet. The Butlins' herd has doubled in the last year, to 15 milking cows. Even so, at less than $10,000, the personal draw for the family is substandard. And that meagre return is contingent upon things working out on the farm as they do on paper. Still, Nina says, "Cream shipping is no worse than anything else in agriculture. It's no more marginal than other commodities, and it's the only thing you can do as a beginning farmer in Nova Scotia and get an income right away."

"Cream shipping hinges on idealism," David says. "Underlying it all is the strong conviction that the principles behind mixed farming — farming that is geared to the supply of local needs and doesn't contribute to overproduction, and is ecologically sound, therefore is not a monoculture type of existence — must one day prove themselves right."

The next morning begins inauspiciously. It is bitterly cold. The last cow in the milking line must be cajoled, kicked and dragged to her feet, only to discover that she has a swollen stifle joint — another veterinary bill. The line to the tractor radiator breaks as David is ploughing the lane. And as we are about to load the cream for market, we discover that the back door to the station wagon is frozen shut.

To balance the ledger: The weaners are spry, the pigs will soon be ready for market, and the milk-fed calves are bearing out their good breeding.

It is five miles from Crackwillow Farm to the Tatamagouche Creamery, which Nina describes as an "island in the storm." David talks as we manoeuvre the icy dirt road. "It's tremendously satisfying to know that you are providing a need for the community. As the price of transportation increases, the importance of locally produced food is going to increase. Butter is one of the most underproduced commodities in Nova Scotia. With the new generation of cream producers, who are looking at it with a lot more emphasis on management and production, presumably we can produce butter as competitively as it can be imported."

The Tatamagouche Creamery now operates at only one-third capacity, even though the province imports 80 per cent of its butter. When we arrive, cream cans are being unloaded from the Valley Truck. Once a week, cream is shipped over 200 miles from the few remaining cream producing farms in the Annapolis Valley to Tatamagouche. In the '40s, six 3-ton trucks were kept busy, every day except Sunday, picking up cream roadside in the local area. For the past 10 years, farmers have had to transport their own cream to market, for which they receive a provincial transportation subsidy of 10 cents per pound.

The numbered cans are weighed on the Toledo scale and a small sample ladled from each for sweetness and butterfat tests, the two indices which determine the creamery premium paid to the producer. Like most new shippers, David transports his cream in five gallon plastic buckets, as the traditional cream cans are no longer available. Replacement parts for separators are equally hard to come by. The closest supplier is in Calgary, Alberta. Today, you are more likely to see a separator gracing a suburban front lawn than to see it in use on a farm.

As David's cream is being weighed in, a fellow shipper confides that he may not be in business for much longer. His application for construction of a new barn has just been turned down by the Farm Loan Board. A few days later, with the dejected look of the unsuccessful applicant still clear in my mind, I questioned loan counsellor, Bob Adams, about the FLB's alleged prejudice against small farms. He answers that there is no policy at the FLB to discourage small farms in general, or cream shippers in particular. He notes that the cream shipper can carry only half the debt load that a shipper of fluid milk (fluid is the milk we drink) can, and that they must advise against overcapitalization: "The last thing we are here for is to get people into trouble."

David has had to overcome his conditioning, as a child growing up in postwar England, that credit is the ruination of a person. He has accepted money as another tool, like a tractor or a spade. For the Butlins, it has been a year of major commitments: an addition to the old barn, acquisition of quality breeding stock and expansion of their land base.

David received one of only two FLB loans made to cream shippers in 1979. He says,"Our experience with the Department has been very good, certainly not antagonistic. We've always been surprised at the support we've unearthed when we presented our case. They just don't think about it. Cream shipping is an idea that has to be promoted."

In Tatamagouche, the Butlins have found the traditional society which they were seeking for themselves and their two preschool children. Also they have close bonds with a community of new-comers. The hundred-strong North Shore Organic Growers' As-sociation provides a ready market for David's organically raised beef and home cured pork. Looking back at B.C., Nina says " It was nothing like being a farmer. You didn't feel like you were going to be carted off at any minute.

"Our vision has always included some kind of apocalypse in our life time, when everything falls apart. And the best place to be is on some land, which hopefully won't be taken away from you."

Charlie Orr is a zealous supporter of cream production. He was a prime mover in the formation of the Cream Producers Associa-tion, and its first president. He argues that Nova Scotia is ill-suited for large agribusiness-type farms, whereas cream production "fits into the scale of things."

I've heard it murmured in bureaucratic quarters that his logic is "insidious." His approach, however, reflects the scientist's objec-tivity. Upon examination of his credentials, this is not surprising: B.A., University of Glasgow, Scotland; M.A., University of Guelph, and Ph. D., post-Doctoral, in Biochemistry, Johns Hopkins, Bal-timore. How an RNA researcher from the venerated halls of Johns

Hopkins ended up championing the cause of the small farmer requires several giant steps in the telling.

Charlie's talk is spiced with his native Scots brogue and a healthy dose of humour. About his undergraduate training in agriculture, he quips, "God knows how I got into agriculture in the beginning. It had something to do with no parental guidance. I thought that I wanted to be out in the fresh air, so I went into agriculture." Far from getting him out in the fresh air, it led him on the path of a professional student. When the research purse strings tightened in 1972, he decided it was time for a change.

To the horror of his academic colleagues, Charlie and his wife Jennie, who was a Research Assistant at Johns Hopkins, headed for the Wild West. The scheme, abetted by the Wyoming Department of Agriculture, was to grow pedigree legume seed on the banks of the Grey Bull River. When the movie makers and television crews arrived, Charlie repented. "If I was going to make a pure ass of myself, I wanted to do it quietly." The Orrs retreated to the East, then to Scotland, where Charlie resumed teaching and bought and refurbished a derelict 1640s cottage, to raise another stake. Within three days of coming out to Nova Scotia to reconnoitre farming prospects, Charlie became the owner of an abandoned North Shore farm. Their troubles were only beginning.

The first year, the Orrs raised sheep but soon found that the cash flow was insufficient for a family of six. A cream cheque seemed the only option. They bought Jerseys "because any bigger cow would have been standing in the gutter." They were getting set up when, on Christmas Day 1974, the old Cumberland barn burned to the ground. They lost their tractor and all of their hay and grain. Fortunately, the animals were saved. The cows were dispersed to neighbouring barns, and the pigs took up residence in the cellar of the house for a noisy, smelly tenure. In the face of financial ruin and the February cold, Charlie began to rebuild, saddled with a second FLB loan.

The time since has been spent bringing back the land, improving breeding stock, and most importantly fine-tuning the use of the skim milk for the feeding of the hogs. In sharp contrast to the willy-nilly methods attributed to the old-time shippers, Charlie has approached the use of his skim milk (which he describes as an almost perfect pig feed) with the discipline learned studying cell membranes. His on-the-farm experiments may serve as a model for

39

other cream shippers. Certainly, they fill the vacuum which currently exists in cream production research in the Department of Agriculture.

"What is difficult is to have the pig numbers tied in with the number of milking cows, so that at all times you have an adequate supply of skim milk. When that's working, I can produce pigs cheaper than anyone in the province," he claims.

But Charlie and Jennie are familiar with the animal inflation factor. Cream shipping farms are small and are likely to remain so, unless there is a quantum leap in the state of the art. The manual separation of the cream and hand feeding of the skim is labour intensive. There is also a limit to the amount of skim milk that can be handled without creating a rancid mess. The Orrs are working toward a 28-cow milking herd, in order to provide an income for their teenage family and to keep creditors off their back. Such a herd size would give the Orrs the option (with the one proviso the quota is available and affordable) to make the switch to fluid. If it were a matter of livelihood, they would; however, they remain determined to demonstrate that cream shipping is "as profitable as any other dairy enterprise." They also are committed to the mixed farming concept.

"It's the only damned way to farm," says Charlie. "Basically, you've got to make the ground produce for you and the only way you can do that is to produce shit.

"I feel quite strongly about this old, tired land here. I'm fundamentally opposed to inorganic fertilizers, because I'm sure that they are destroying the health of our soils. I'm sure the bacteria cannot survive that localized acidity.

"If you destroy that health in your soil, you are basically just farming hydroponically. You've got a dead substrate out there. You have to let nature help you. The ground is the legacy we have to look after."

Charlie admits that finding new caretakers of the land will not be easy: "There's no glamour associated with being a cream shipper and that's a major drawback. But the glamour comes when it's shown that it's profitable.

"It doesn't seem to be a mental block for a young fellow to assume a debt of $150,000, but then he hasn't assumed that kind of debt before. It's bandied about rather freely in the agricultural

40

bureaucracy that it's the kind of debt one can handle; it's an intolerable burden."

The cows are milked, the hogs fed. Jennie has separated the cream, attended to the calves and her personal pride, two handsome Brown Swiss heifers that she brought into the herd from Connecticut. She excuses herself, it's 9:30, bedtime. Charlie and I sit beside the kitchen stove for a last round of tea. The muscled forearms, projecting from the frayed ends of his long-sleeved undershirt, are of a man far removed from the lecture theatre and the glass world of the lab. My question probes his day's end tiredness, for any tag end of regret.

"It's a great family operation. These kids have learned one hell of a lot more than if I had been a prof. They are different kids, smarter kids. They understand the value of a dollar, which I never did at their age. And they've seen life and death, which is hard at first.

"The family is always working together. It can't work if there's any friction or problem there. You soon know whether the relationship is sound or not. You have to be totally dedicated. Otherwise, you're not going to make it."

Charles and Judith Hubbard are also immigrants. Reluctant converts to cream production, they are now steadfast supporters. Their farms are near Northport, Cumberland County. On one side of the road is a garishly orange, steel-sided barn: This is Charles' domain, a modern farrow-to-finish operation. Opposite, on the home side of the road, is the big weathered barn where Judith houses her herd of Jerseys. Their setup offers a rare opportunity to compare, side by side, modern agribusiness practice with the traditional small farm philosophy.

Born in England, their honeymoon in a Welsh cottage led to their becoming farmsteaders on a 40-acre holding. A neighbour in the all-Welsh-speaking community christened Charles' first sow, "Mother Hubbard." They bought several cows, and the pigs increased over time. Also the family grew. Judith recalls, "The arrival of four children, one after another, limited my usefulness in the barn." Finally, their ambition outgrew the homestead potential. Returning to England, they had to settle for an even smaller holding of five acres and an affiliation with a cooperatively owned hog A.I.-unit. The unit prospered, but the Hubbards still dreamed of their own land base.

When they arrived on Nova Scotia's North Shore in the late 1960s farms were for sale "two for a penny." The purchase of 800 acres satisfied their yen for land, but for new farmers, it was disconcerting to find themselves stepping into a vacuum. "There was no one to follow," says Charles. "There were very few people here doing anything." His contacts in England helped to get them started. Today, Charles is considered one of Nova Scotia's premier swine breeders, and his gross income places him in the 95th percentile of provincial producers.

The more modest cream side of the balance sheet came about at the behest of a neighbour. Pat Darragh was a retired dairyman who worked for Charles. "He told us that we'd never be able to put the farm on its feet unless we had cattle. Of course, he was right," says Judith, "because we had the land — and all those stupid pigs over there — and were not using it. We began to listen to him, and we decided eventually to go into cream production and have Jersey cows, which, in fact, was what I always wanted."

After defending his "stupid pigs," Charles continues: "When we got the cows, we were able to use the grain we were growing. You can look at it from the point of view that it is the cows now that we are using as a converter of pork meat from grass."

Charles' side of the road has remained tied into the use of imported, pelleted grain. However, there is an interchange between the two farms. Judith's barn has become an infirmary of sorts. "We bring over his disaster cases," Judith says. "And we can very often save their lives."

Charles picks up on the point and the humour: "It's just incredible. It seems silly to say it, because all we're doing is repeating what great-grandfather would have said 60 years ago. But so many of these modern people have forgotten what great-grandfather said.

"We brought 20 pigs over — we literally brought them over, because they were unable to travel under their own steam. The first lot we brought over, none of them died. Within a short time, they were in pretty good shape. In fact one day when we came down the hill from the church (Judith had left the door open) the whole darn lot were running all over the place. You never would have believed that they were the lot who couldn't even walk here."

In addition to its medicinal value, Charles believes that the skim milk increases the margin per cow by 50 per cent. "Some would say that the value of the skim is 10 or 15 cents per gallon. That is not the way to look at it. The end product is 50 cents worth of meat - that's what you get paid for."

The cows have made it possible for the Hubbards to put into practice the principles of their European grounding in agriculture: Production must be founded on its land base. There must be a direct relationship between livestock units and acres involved. Charles does not see these principles being practised in Nova Scotia.

"Some of our finest units are based on acres from the West. In essence, the majority of the livestock units are manufacturing units. They are not farming units in the traditional sense.

" The stupid form of thought says that the only type of production is based on cheap energy and the quantity per unit. None of this is related to the amount of production per acre, which is the way they teach things in Europe. That's why we feel the cows and work that Judith is doing is so important, as much as it's a totally different system. Of the two, the cream side will last longer. I'm not worried about profits, but about principles. And as things change this side, the cream, will be in existence much longer."

The signs of change cannot be ignored: skyrocketing energy, fertilizer and machinery costs and the tenuous production of those Western acres, where the organic matter of the soils is being depleted by monoculture. Nevertheless, Charles is given the well-intentioned advice to worry about nothing except the pigs and their production per unit. And Judith must endure the patronizing attitude that she is dabbling in cream production as an amusement, one she can afford because of the other side of the road. "Little do they realize," says Charles, who is weathering the bottoming out of the pork market, "that the only money we're living on at the moment is the cream money." When pork prices are better, the Hubbards continue to sacrifice their bottom line to build up a complete farm.

Charles views the status quo as a kind of Tower of Babylon, with the farmer as the column supporting an outsized superstructure. "On the far side of the road, being highly capital-intensive and very largely dependent upon borrowing monies, we are in practice supporting an awful lot of people in one form or another. On this side of the road, we are supporting very few people.

"The farms would be all right but the system would break down if we all reverted to this [cream] side of the road. All those who are dependent on the present system, which is based on cheap energy, would suddenly find themselves flat on their faces. You can see where the vested interests are."

Charles gets incensed about cost of production figures and meaningless statistics, like the one which classifies his side of the road as a "Superfarm." He has calculated that his working wage is less than what his 19-year old son can make at a summer job in the nearby town of Amherst. To compound the irony and insult, Charles alone produces enough pork to supply half of the demand of Amherst's 9,000 inhabitants.

"Someone has to say to these idiots, 'Look! One man cannot look after more than a certain amount, and while we're insisting on a relatively reasonable society, which involves certain standards, therefore, holidays or leave or number of hours worked, then stop fooling around with these things, because the only reason for doing so is to try to come up with a cost of production per unit.' They should be decent enough to put these criteria into the cost of production formula, and not continue to assume one man can do more and more in a given time. There are limits which, over-reached, will cause the whole system to collapse, where the next generation will not take over the family farm. Then you will have expensive foods."

For the consumer, Charles believes that there is security only in farm numbers. " For the North Shore, the farming of the future will be compact little units, which probably one man can handle; no more than 30 cows or 30 or 40 sows — with its acreage behind it feeding that unit and machinery innovations to adapt to its climate."

The school bus has arrived. The Hubbard children (there are seven) clamour into the back porch, pausing only long enough to deposit their lunchboxes and to grab their skates. Charles disappears to his duties across the road. There is time for a brief tour. The barn is well lit and clean, the Jerseys surprisingly diminutive when one is used to a milking line of Holsteins. Kittens and spotted pups roll about in the hay.

Judith and I stand at the back door of the barn. The children, who look like little figures in a Breughel painting, are skating where a depression in the pasture has made a natural rink. Horses and ponies canter about the field. The brow of the hill is ploughed in rippling rows, ready for next year's grain. I remark on the sombre beauty of Nova Scotia, which, as a native, I am congenitally attached to. "I didn't think so at first," Judith rejoins, "but yes, it is beautiful."

Most people native to the North Shore have cream shipping in their background. Those old enough witnessed the emigration from farms, precipitated and accelerated by World War II. Of the young men who came back from overseas, many did not return to the farms. Many who stayed on the farm during the war were shunted into war-related industries, such as the Pictou shipyards and the Trenton carworks and gun shop. Better industrial wages continued to lure people off the family farm in the 50's and 60's. Today, thousands of acres of land that once produced cream lie idle, at the mercy of alder and pasture spruce, and consequently there is a dearth of father-son cream shipping farms.

One is Blockhouse Farm, which takes its name from Fort Franklin, built on the site in 1763 to guard the entrance to Tatamagouche Bay. A Golden Guernsey sign hangs at the roadside. Looking down the long lane, one would guess that this is a prosperous farm, though it is far from ostentatious. The large hip-backed house has a new coat of white paint with red trim. The outbuildings and barn are painted to match. The straw stubble, bristling through a light cover of snow, adds to the general impression of tidiness and comfort.

Baillie Ferguson's father bought the 200-acre farm in 1919. At age 22, Baillie's only son, Keith, is assuming more responsibility on the place. He will be the third Ferguson generation to ship cream to the Tatamagouche plant.

The redolence of deep-frying doughnuts wafts from the kitchen when Baillie comes to greet me on the back porch. For the past few months he has been convalescing from major surgery. When well he plies his carpenter's trade part time (as did my own father). "I had to get sick to have a vacation," he says, as we sit down at the kitchen table.

Baillie is forthright. He wonders out loud how new farmers can undertake rapid expansion and finance the purchase of purebred cows. When he started into farming, he says, "I didn't have money to invest and I wasn't going into debt. I always figured that I was going to own my own little manure pile and if I wanted to quit, I could quit, and call everything my own."

Because of the debt load, he has never entertained a changeover to fluid. Before there was a government support for butter, the fluid shippers were "besting" him, but today, he can say, "I figure that we're as well off as milk shippers, because we don't have as big an overhead to carry. The stuff we can get by with, we can come out at the end of the year with as much to show as the milk producer."

Of large farms, he says, "It's not as rosy as it looks." The Fergusons have a ready market for their weaners and veal, grow their own grain and, as Keith says, " The cows give enough to fill the pail." Unlike the new shippers that have had to start from scratch, Keith will not have a debt load on his shoulders. Like his father, he will be able to farm to suit himself.

As we're drinking coffee over a plate of Mrs. Ferguson's delicious doughnuts, a neighbour drops in to ask after Baillie's health. He is introduced as a one-time shipper. As for so many, there was no one who wanted to take over the farm.

Baillie leans forward, his arms resting on the table: "I often wonder who is going to do the farming after the generation of my age is done. They're still not getting many young fellows encouraged. There's not the profit in it for them, that's the trouble. I've preached that for years that they can't let the land go back to the woods, because the population is increasing and the farmers are getting less."

He reflects for a moment, "I may never see it, but there's going to be nothing to eat."

EXHIBITION TIME IN OX COUNTRY

In the 1950s, when I was a member of a 4-H Club, I got a week off school in September to attend Exhibition. Since then, whenever I return to agricultural fairgrounds, I am seized by a sense of time stolen, of delicious leisure. This feeling is heightened by the fact that while the world has changed dramatically, exhibitions have remained very much the same.

The familiarity is reassuring: a larder of prize-winning pickles and baked goods is, alas, as inviting to the palate as to the eye; yards of handcrafts have been stitched, quilted, knitted, crocheted, tatted, hooked, then embroidered, smocked and appliqued into a lame of colour and practical design; and familiar patterns like Log Cabin are draped beside such modern mutants as Urban Sprawl. There are piglets and ponies — always a delight — as well as poultry in an improbable array of colours, shapes and exotic plumages. There are the livestock barns: cow barns; horse barns (light and heavy); sheep and swine barns and ox barns.

Three decades after my introduction to this festival of rural culture, I find myself on the fairgrounds of the South Shore Exhibition in Bridgewater, Nova Scotia. The Big Ex, as promoters like to call it, is the first of fourteen such fairs held throughout the province each summer, and one of the biggest.

I am but one of 70,000 who will pass through the gate by Saturday. On this, a Monday morning, I look happily to the week ahead and think of reacquainting myself with the animals, the showmanship, the artistry and the conviviality of rural society. In particular, I am anticipating an opportunity to partake of the spectacle of strength and will which is ox pulling. In Bridgewater as elsewhere in western Nova Scotia — in "ox-country" — the ox-pulls are the fair's most popular attraction.

I have loved ox pulling since childhood when I was introduced to this workingman's sport. In 1957, I sat in the exhibition building in Yarmouth, Nova Scotia watching what was billed as the World Championship Ox Haul. As the pyramid of 200-pound weights grew higher on the drag so did the tension in the crowd. Each teamster, satisfied that enough weight had been added, settled into position between the heads of his team of patient oxen. Grasping a horn with one hand and twirling his whip in a circle above the team's back with the other, he let out with a resounding command — "Hauuuuul!" — and the oxen responded with a mighty thrust of their immense shoulders. The drag moved forward — grudgingly, inexorably, heroically.

That simple invocation, which melds man and animal to a common purpose, still stirs my blood as much now as it did the first time I heard it. And I will hear it many times over the next few days. The variety of pulling contests will culminate in The Oland's International Ox Pull on Friday night, in which four Canadian teams will compete against four teams from the United States for the Oland's Cup.

But on Monday morning, the excitement and the crowds seem far away. There is time now to wander the grounds, to inspect the barns, to settle in and savour. I drink in the familiar sights and sounds and inhale the good smells — among which, as country-born, I count the earthiness of fresh dung. The best time of day at the Exhibition, in my opinion, is morning, when the exhibitors are about their business of watering and feeding, currying coats and braiding tails, or, like myself, simply admiring what the land and hard work have wrought. There is time now for casual talk before the crowds begin to pour in and the Ferris wheel begins to spin. Then, the Exhibition takes on a carnival spirit, with the frenzy, the bright lights, and the sounds of the city. Of course, that, too, is part of the fun and offers a welcome change for many of the country people who come here on a busman's holiday. For now, however, people's minds are on the show ring and the reward of ribbons, which by week's end will fly from one end of the barns to the other like flags on the halyards of a ship.

By mid-morning, a peaceful lull has fallen over the exhibition grounds. Sound travels cleanly and clearly through the air, and the most peaceful of those sounds is the nostalgic tok-tok-tok of the ox bells as the teams are taken out for their morning walk.

I follow the sound to the far corner of the fair grounds, where 70 teams are housed in the two barns. Nowhere —except perhaps in the heavy horse barns — is so much care lavished upon the animals. A teamster takes great pride in the appearance of his team. To begin with, he tries to match a pair. Often he must travel throughout his district to find a match for a steer in his own herd — one of the same breed, build and, if possible, with similar markings.

Many teamsters prefer a crossbred ox. Hereford and Red Durham is a popular choice: the Hereford blood produces a good looking, white-faced ox; Durham provides "the spark" for pulling as well as a "spreckle" of red colour. A yoke, painted red or blue, hangs above each pair of stalls, as does a name plaque. With few exceptions, the plaques read "Bright & Lion," the traditional South Shore names for oxen.

This morning, the teams are being yoked and paraded through the show ring to be judged in the categories Best Decorated and Best Pair. After judge Elzee Saulnier finishes his slow military perusal of the teams, like a sergeant major inspecting the troops, I join him in the shade of his ringside booth. I ask him what he looks for in a pair of oxen. "If I'm lookin' for a pair of oxen for myself I'd like to have a mated pair of oxen," Saulnier says in his French Shore accent. "Both look alike, both the same size, both travel the same in the yoke — we call that loose travellin'. They don't look like they're all humped up and their head down.

"And I like to see a nice set of horns on a pair of cattle. That's one of the main things because you meet people and you're always head on."

Those who meet a team of oxen head on see a pair of rather doleful and surprisingly pretty animals bound together by a wooden yoke. Yoke makers (a disappearing breed) prefer yellow birch for its toughness; with a saw, adze and drawknife, they shape the yoke to fit comfortably over the neck of the ox. To complete the fit, they gouge out grooves called horn boxes, into which the horns fit precisely. "Yoke's got to fit the ox like the shoe's got to fit your foot," one teamster told me. Each yoke is custom built and, when finished, looks something like a crude, heavy bow. Teamsters yoke the animals by winding about twenty feet of leather strapping around the horns and into grooves, called strap gains, at either end of the yoke. In the pulling ring, they attach the shaft of the drag to the yoke, making the connection between beast and burden.

As important as the functional paraphernalia are the decorative accoutrements. Each ox has a head pad. Traditionally, the head-pads are "brassed up" with hearts, diamonds and shamrocks, and further embellished with rhinestones. Finally, each member of a team must have a neck strap for an oxbell, the source of the pastoral music of the ox barn.

The oxen, thus adorned, are the star performers at the Big Ex. On Tuesday, the day of the Grand Street Parade, many of the teams are yoked and teamed through the streets of downtown Bridgewater, re-creating a scene that might have been commonplace a century ago. I station myself on the last leg of the parade loop, which leads up a steep hill from the LaHave River to the fair grounds.

First to pass is the town crier, clanging his bell and looking uncomfortable in his heavy frock coat and fur-trimmed, three cornered hat. Black Percherons, nostrils flaring, and Shriners on mini-bikes, climb the torturously steep incline. Waves of marching bands roll up the street, now awash with boots, kilts and khaki. White furry hats, like tufts of cotton candy, appear above a rise. Soon, majorettes twirl and toss their batons while queens and princesses for a day wave greetings from convertibles. Floats, pulled by every conceivable conveyance from draft horses to Mack trucks, advertise the charity of local service clubs and the products of local entrepreneurs. The parade presents the community in cross-section, and no one, it seems, wants to be conspicuous by his or her absence. The town's major employer, Michelin Tire, flies the motto, "Pulling Together," in clever deference to the region's symbol of progress and hard work. Last up the hill, in the position of honour, are the ox teams themselves, sure and steady of pace and unbothered by the heat or hoopla.

Oxen were a vital part of pioneer life in Nova Scotia and had some distinct advantages over the horse. First, they were cheap to feed, often grazing on marginal marshland that produced a wild crop of salt hay. The slow steady pace of the ox resulted in less damage to farm implements than occurred with draft horses, which tend to be quicker or, as teamsters say, "sharper." And when they

50

became too old to work, oxen offered one final advantage over horses — they could be eaten by the farm family.

Horses eventually replaced oxen in most of Nova Scotia, but the ox held sway on the South Shore. Surefooted, they were better suited for the rocky coast, where they were put to work hauling seaweed for fertilizer, pulling fish catches from weirs, and winching boats ashore — all unsuitable tasks for the more temperamental horses. Of course, the ox cart was a popular form of personal transportation, and convoys of them often made the long haul from inland communities to the coast.

For three centuries a dominant force in community life, oxen had all but disappeared from the rural landscape 30 years ago. It was then that a group of teamsters got together to form the Maritime Ox-pulling Association. It proved the salvation of the ox and, in the process, turned a pleasant pastime into a formal and popular sport.

One of those instrumental in reviving interest in the ox was Gordon Lohnes, a founding member of the association. A tall, lanky man with a makem cigarette stuck permanently on his lower lip, Lohnes is something of a father figure to the younger generation of teamsters. I have to arrive at the fairgrounds early in the morning to catch him before his daily work of supervising the show rings gets into full swing.

"Years ago they was pulling but at the time, they used to use the oxen. Now, most generally," Gordon says, softening his "r's" and speaking in the distinctive South Shore drawl, "we just keep them for the hobby of ox-pulling, you see. So that's the reason the association was formed to keep the oxen going.

"You could see it coming up. If we didn't do something the oxen was going to go the other way. Now we got more people interested in the oxen that really don't need them any more than I do. But they just keep them because they like them."

Thanks to Lohnes and others like him, the ox has made a remarkable recovery. Today, the South Shore Exhibition is the only place in the province — or anywhere else, for that matter — where onlookers can see 100 or more yoked cattle.

For me the patient strength of oxen symbolizes the struggle to maintain rural traditions. Though the ox is no longer an essential component of a working farm, the people in ox country have been steadfast in their loyalty to the animal that built the country. They were not content, in a pragmatic gesture to modernity, merely to cast the ox aside as redundant. And they continue to show due respect for the ox with their painstaking attention to the look of the team.

Ox pulling honours the ox by giving it work. For those of us watching the ox pull, we see how man and animal can become a unit. Just as the oxen are yoked together, man and animal are bound in a heroic struggle when the teamster takes hold of a horn and asks them to "Haul!" It is good to be reminded of this relationship upon which rural society was founded.

Tuesday night is reserved for the Canadian Qualifying Ox Pull, which will decide the four teams to compete against the Americans on Friday. The plodding teams enter the ring to the incongruous rhythm of *Bo Diddley,* performed by Rompin' Ronnie Hawkins, who is just finishing his set in the adjacent outdoor arena. Ox Pulling is a sport with a loyal following, and fans here are knowledgable in the way hockey fans are at the Montreal Forum. I have the good fortune to sit beside an aspiring young teamster, who provides a running commentary on the herculean spectacle in the ring.

The teams pull in turns. Each has three tries to pull a 5000-pound drag a distance of six feet, after which more weight is added. The four teams to pull the heaviest load will qualify. To begin with the drag is on a cement slab. "It's a dead pull off concrete, there's no give," my interpreter tells me. "That drag seems to weld to the slab."

"Get up Lion, Gee, Gee. Step up Lion," shouts one unsuccessful contestant.

"They say teamin'," my friend confides, "but you're only teamin' the weak ox."

Of the 39 teams, fewer than half move the drag the required six feet. There are heroic victories and failures. The crowd responds appropriately with cheers, applause or good-natured jibes. "He can't team. He couldn't ride a bicycle," a spectator comments, when one teamster slides in under the horns of his struggling team and lands ingloriously on his behind.

Teamsters display individual styles. Kendall Oickle, whose team moves the drag on the first try, is quiet and reassuringly unhurried. He never makes a quick or untoward movement or raises his voice above a whisper — and his team seems to respond in like style, quietly doing their job.

Others team with emotional fervour. Donnie Travis of Yarmouth County is one such high-pitched performer and, hence, a real crowd pleaser. Travis seems to be as much in communication with the bleachers as with his own team. "He should be a wrestler," says a voice behind me.

Travis wears his ball cap backwards and sports a tank top that shows his bronzed and muscled upper body to good effect. When the team fails to respond on its first try, he throws the cap into the dirt and kicks it like an irate baseball manager making a point with an impassive umpire. Regaining his composure, he stalks around the team, shortens the chain connecting the yoke to the drag, kicks away gravel in front of the drag, then ducks down, putting his head between the two oxen for a tete-a-tete, delivered in unctuous, audible tones.

"I said listen to me. Whoa, Lion, back haw. Now we got to haul. Now, Spark, haul!

"Come on, Spark, Lion. Bring it up heeeere!"

The team pulls the drag forward the required six feet, Elzee Saulnier nods his head, and Travis throws his whip into the air to the wild applause of the crowd. To everyone's surprise, including Travis's, it seems, he has qualified.

Last up is Darrel Watkins. Of all the entrants, Watkins is my personal favourite. I grew up watching his father haul and then Watkins himself take over where his father left off — winning consistently and with style. Now, Watkins's own son, Darren, is capable of beating his father, keeping the winning tradition alive.

Win or lose, Watkins brings to ox-pulling a riveting style. Other teamsters watch him to learn his secrets. "He's a smart cookie," one teamster tells me with grudging respect. "He knows just when to add on weight, and when to rest them to get a second wind. And he'll get three starts to your one. He'll be yelling 'Whoa,' but he'll be jiggin' that drag around — you gotta watch him." And watch him you do. The audience can't seem to take their eyes off him as he puts his team through their paces. He is a dervish of energy — circling, chiding, fidgeting — every action designed to concentrate the attention of the team on the task at hand, pulling the 3 1/2 tons of deadweight. Still, nothing distinguishes Watkins's style more than his voice. When he invokes his cattle to "Haul," he not only stirs the seemingly somnolent cattle into action, it is as if he disturbs the gods in their heaven.

I delight in his histrionics. He crouches with his hands on his knees and speaks to the cattle, eye to eye, in the teamster's equivalent of a mound conference. He "Whoas" the team back, flicking his whip at their knees; then, without warning, the Watkins's yell begins, rising up through his thin-legged, barrel-chested frame and issuing from a gaping mouth like a wind storm. His voice gains steadily in volume — "Hauuuu..." —his whip twirls above the team's head like the cone of a twister, the oxen hoof the dirt, their heavy shoulders heave forward in unison; Watkins's voice reaches a hoarse crescendo — "....uuul!" The drag slides forward but stops short of the mandatory six feet.

Watkins clamps his mouth shut and cocks his head to one side in an attitude of dismay, as if to say, "Come on, guys, what do you think we're doing out here?" He then asks the drag attendant to unhitch the team, making me wonder if he is all finished. I should know better. It is all part of the strategy. As he takes the team for a little promenade, he exhorts them quietly. Circling the team back between the rails, he backs them up, crowding them against the drag so that when they move forward they will have to lunge, uncoiling their power — and, in the process, will jerk the load into motion, overcoming the inertia of the drag against concrete. Again the yell from his heels, but this time Watkins backs up quickly, making the team come to him. And they do, bringing the drag forward the balance of six feet. To no one's surprise, Watkins qualifies for an unprecedented twelfth time and will join Travis, Kendall Oickle, and Leon Corkum in the ring on Friday night against the Americans.

The next day, I seek out Darrel Watkins to talk to him about the passion and skill he displays as a teamster. To me it is a privilege and, yes, to borrow the sportscaster's parlance, "a thrill," to talk to a man I have watched and admired for thirty years. He is a hero in the sense that he embodies what is best in his sport — a sport that has a cultural validity in this corner of the world as nowhere else.

"I fell through the ice when I was five years old," Watkins begins his story. "There was a little air hole behind me, and I remember my brother, with a friend, was ahead of me on the ice, and he said, 'Watch out for that hole.' I was just this little kid, but I can

54

remember looking for that hole, and I was gradually slidin' backwards on my skates. First thing, I went into it.

"They hauled me out of there and I was soaking wet and cold. I went up to the house — up over the hill, across the railway track, over the field and into the house. The next thing I remember is asking my mother how many more exhibitions I was going to see. I thought I was going to die, eh, and that's all I was worried about. So I had this in me all my life I guess."

I want to know how Watkins does what he does so well.

"It's got to come natural," he says. " Probably some things I don't know I'm doin'. I've worked a lot in the woods and around the barn, and after a while, you pick up certain ways an animal responds to. Someone who just comes and buys a pair of oxen doesn't develop that kind of feeling."

Almost all teamsters speak of the rapport between animal and human. This finely-tuned relationship is a mysterious and fragile thing. Trying to make oxen haul a load when they are neither ready nor able is called "hanging the team," and it is the surest way to break a team's spirit. In the way that oxen in an ideal team ideally would match each other in appearance and strength, the spirit of the animals and the temperament of the teamster must be a good match.

I spend hours observing this relationship in action, as there are pulls morning, evening and night for the various weight classes. One noon hour, with the temperature hovering around 30 degrees Celsius, I sit in the bleachers with the wives of teamsters, the only other people in the sun.

"They're not true ox people," says Janet Sabean, gesturing dismissively toward the open door of the ox barns where the men have taken shelter from the heat. "They're in the shade, we're in the sun. We can see whether they made their three feet where they can't. They sit there and argue about it."

The women laugh with a conspiratorial glee.

"They get into arguments in the winter on how much they pulled and where they placed, and then we get out the books," says Barbara Hurlburt, indicating a little black book in her lap. Hurlburt records every pull: the weight pulled, the number of tries to do it, and the percentage of the team's weight versus the weight of the drag.

"When you sit here all day," she says, "it makes it more interesting to keep statistics."

Women are not just dedicated fans who sit in the mid-day sun and travel every weekend in the summer. Many of them have taken to teaming and have proven themselves more than a match for men in the ring.

"We hold our own," says Connie. "I've beat Donnie several times."

As Friday dawns the question on everybody's mind is whether the Canadians will be a match for the Americans. The Bridgewater pull is the first half of a home-and-home series. The same eight teams will meet again in New Cumberland, Maine, in September. In Bridgewater, they pull American style, a so-called Distance Pull. The winner is the team that pulls a pre-determined weight the furthest distance in five minutes. In Maine, the teams will pull Canadian style. There, each team will have three tries to pull a load a distance of three feet, at which time more weight is added. Under the Canadian system, the team that pulls the greatest weight wins. First held in 1957, these international contests have fanned a friendly rivalry. Usually the hometown crowds have little to cheer about, however, as the Americans usually beat the Canadians in Canada, and vice-versa.

One look at the American oxen reveals why they are better suited to the distance pull. They are, for the most part, Holstein steers, taller and longer in the legs than the more compact, lower-to-the-ground beef cattle breeds that are preferred —primarily for their looks — by the Canadians. The American oxen dwarf the Canadian teams, so much so that they suggest the epic stature of Paul Bunyan's blue ox Babe.

There are other differences between American and Canadian oxen. Americans employ a neck yoke, a beam with a bow which passes under the neck of the ox, so that their teams are said to pull from the neck rather than from the head as Canadian teams do. As a rule, the yoke is unpainted and Americans dispense with head pads, collar and oxbells. To me the American oxen are pragmatic beasts in practical clothing.

However homely, the American ox is well chosen "to walk to victory" in the distance pull. But the stockier Canadian teams, with their lower centre of gravity, are better adapted to pull heavier loads in the Canadian style pull. Watkins, for example, has won seven times in Maine, while victory in the international pull has eluded him.

Rain delays the pull until Saturday evening, when the bleachers begin to fill two hours before the pull. By 7:30, 6000 people have assembled to greet the contestants. The Americans enter the ring first, flying the Stars and Stripes from their yokes, followed by the host teams, which answer with the Maple Leaf. The national anthems blare from the loudspeakers and are absorbed by the sound of the midway.

A draw determines the sequence of teams to pull; the weight has been set at 6,400 pounds, a load heavy enough to give the Canadians some hope of winning. That slim hope seems to vanish when Deane Anderson's team, a truly massive duo of Holstein-Chianina cross and the pre-pull favourites, quite literally walks away with the three-ton-plus drag. At the five-minute mark, the team has pulled the load a prodigious 331' 5" — nearly 100 feet further than his Canadian predecessor, Kendall Oickle.

The last teamster to pull is Darrel Watkins. His team, breaking with Canadian tradition, is unmatched. Like the Americans, Watkins is primarily interested in how the animals pull, not how they look. And pull they do, at first, responding to Darrel's invocations like a team with real spark in them. They make the turn of the 200-foot course in two minutes, and it appears they have a chance of catching the Americans. But one ox begins to balk, and Watkins, try as he may, is unable to work his usual magic. He comes up well short, at 229 feet 3 inches, good enough for fifth place. Kendall Oickle, at 240 feet 9 inches, cops fourth place and saves face for the Canadian contingent by preventing a clean sweep of the top four spots by the Americans.

After the presentation ceremony, I seek out Watkins to ask how he feels about his performance. He shakes his head, flashes his bright smile and says, "There's always next year."

Like Watkins, I, too, find solace in the knowledge that there will be exhibitions, big and small, throughout rural Nova Scotia, this summer and for many summers to come — and that oxen will be there to delight the crowds.

STORMING THE SAND CASTLES

Around St. Peters Bay, as almost everywhere on Prince Edward Island, the land eases gently into the water. In late May, seaside fields seem preternaturally green. Across the blue corrugations of the bay, red tillage ripples from farmhouses to the water's edge. Hardedged strokes of unsullied colour: green, red, blue. Brakes of softwood border well-ordered fields that march off over rolling hills. Even to a casual tourist, this is a homey, knowable landscape. For me, the Island never fails to work its verdant mesmerism.

Every summer, 122,000 Islanders share this pastoral birthright with 600,000 tourists like myself who ferry across the Northumberland Strait to The Garden of the Gulf. Tourism ranks third behind farming and fishing in the Island economy. Even so, it is not so surprising that some Islanders who cherish peace and quiet view the tourist boon with mixed feelings. That has always been the case. As *The Garden Transformed,* a recent study of Island society, reveals:"Like the Anne [of Green Gables] novels, Island history has both a sense of ambivalence about bucolic isolation and a love/hate relationship with the outside world." Life on a small island has inured a simple truth: islanders value land more than anything.

One theory holds that such sentiment has its origins two centuries ago in the Island's unfortunate history of absentee landlordism. In the 1760's after the British had assumed control of Isle of St. Jean, as they called it, the entire landmass was divided into townships that became personal fiefdoms for friends of Whitehall. Some believe that the loathing ingrained in Island yeoman toward outside control of their land persists to this day, that it has become part of the collective unconscious of contemporary Islanders. Academic myth? Perhaps. But the Island's reaction to the persistent efforts of a group of West Coast developers to build a 1,500-acre $40 million residential/recreational complex — modern-day leisure colony — on the shores of St. Peters Bay suggests that there is more than a little truth to the theory. Indeed, the proposal has sparked a controversy that has raged for two decades now.

In 1970, Robert Evans, president of H.W. Dickie Limited — a Duncan, British Columbia, real estate firm — flew over the north shore of Prince Edward Island. In place of a patchwork of old farms on the Greenwich Peninsula bordering St. Peters Bay, he envisaged a 200-unit hotel/motel, 400 town houses, a championship golf course, an airstrip and a marina. In 1971, he purchased the Cyril Sanderson place, a 500-acre farm at the tip of the peninsula that included a large sand-dune system jutting into the Gulf of St. Lawrence. The next year, he bought two more farms nearby.

In November 1972, however, the Liberal government of Alex Campbell cancelled one of these purchases — the Leith Sanderson property — and made a sweeping amendment to the Real Property Act that limited nonresident purchases to 10 acres without cabinet approval. The measure was seen as a response to fears that speculators, encountering the new legislation protecting the Gulf Islands in British Columbia, had earmarked Prince Edward Island as their new haven. Evans' plans were further frustrated, when the dune system was designated as an environmental protection area in 1975. Despite these setbacks, Evans and his partners — two businessmen from British Columbia and two from Seattle, Washington — have doggedly continued to pursue their plans.

For the Islanders, meanwhile, the Greenwich development has become a focal point for all that ails the Island psyche. To environmentalists, it poses a threat to a unique, pristine, sand dune system. Traditionalists see it as a symbol of the fraying of rural fabric on the Island. To others, it represents a hope for revitalizing an economic backwater and a progressive shift in attitude toward tourism. The issue has divided the cabinet, the community and even households. I first learned of the controversy in May 1984 and, as a longtime Island devotee, decided to visit St. Peters Bay to try to understand the passions that the land inspires in Island hearts.

St. Peters Bay is a seven-mile-long inlet on Prince Edward Island's north shore, 18 miles from Charlottetown, the capital. The bay shelters three communities. At its head is the 19th century shipbuilding centre of St. Peters, a hamlet composed of gabled and mansard-roof houses, a gas station, a general store and two imposing wooden churches for 320 parishioners.

The community of Greenwich strings out along the peninsula that forms the north shore of the bay. Although it was once a thriving farming area, two decades of decline are now evidenced in its big hay barns,their strong backs broken by disuse, and its houses, their grey faces masked by the saplings of the once-proud homestead silver poplars gone to riot. The road ends at the Greenwich dune.

On the south side of the bay is the village of Morell (population 350) and the Red Head Wharf, its economic hub. By midday, the U-shaped wharf shelters the colourful lobster fleet: white, blue, lime-green and lavender long-liners returned from the day's fishing, which began at sunrise. Women in hair nets and men in white peaked caps come and go from the two fish packing plants. Morell is a vital, bustling community, the centre of the modern-day fishery, and St. Peters casts an envious eye toward the village, for it has usurped St. Peters' patriarchal position in the bay.

"In the coves of the land, all things are discussed," wrote Prince Edward Island poet Milton Acorn in "Island," and it was to the coves of the land that I went to hear what St. Peters Bay residents had to say about the development. At one of my early stops, at Cable Head West — north and east of Greenwich — I met Norbert Palmer and LeRoy MacKenzie, two fishermen who had spent the day netting gaspereaux, a herring-like fish used locally as lobster bait. Palmer's truck sat on a deserted beach that stretched to a vanishing point in the direction of the Greenwich dune: to the leisure-minded, a splendid vista; to the locals, a place of work.

I listened as Palmer and MacKenzie talked in the truck cab and wondered how many times such a conversation had been repeated at the general store, on the wharf and in farmhouse kitchens — wherever the question of the Greenwich development raised its head like some kind of exotic perennial plant. It was obvious that the two resented control of a common area by an outsider. It threatened their sense of freedom.

"Why do they want to put a tourist attraction in a place like that?" MacKenzie asked. "Why can't they leave it like it is? I don't want anybody telling me where I can and can't go."

"Mucky-mucks," Palmer snorted, using the local epithet for the well-heeled tourists the development has been designed to attract.

Others are less concerned with the common good than with the threat the development represents to the land itself. Although the Greenwich wetland and dune system has sustained traditional local use — hunting, trapping, fishing — for nearly 200 years, it nevertheless remains one of the least altered natural environments on the largely agrarian and densely settled Island. That fact makes its cause dear to those like Daryl Guignion who feel a need to commune with uncultivated nature. Guignion, a wildlife biologist who agreed to guide me through the dune, lives near Morell and came to Prince Edward Island 17 years ago. "We, as Islanders, deserve a few sites to enjoy and to be able to say to our children, 'This is what it was like,'"he said, as we drove the Greenwich Road.

As we passed the Cyril Sanderson place, Guignion spotted a red fox, surprised by our downwind arrival, its bright back a giveaway in the green grass. "It's a tremendous area for foxes because of the small mammals," explained Guignion. Meadow voles and jumping mice inhabit the dune, and deer mice, shrews and redbacked voles find their niches in the adjacent woodland.

The leading edge of the dune rose up ahead of us, a solid white wave travelling inland at the dreamlike pace of 10 to 20 feet per year, now breaking silently on a summer field, inexorably drowning it. Dead tops of white birch stuck up through the sand like gothic candelabra gracing an immense white tablecloth.

The Greenwich system is a wandering dune, making it unique to Prince Edward Island and a rarity along the Eastern Seaboard, where most dune systems have been stabilized. It is this distinction that makes it so important to those who, like Guignion, are concerned with preserving the natural heritage of the province.

We ambled through the undulating landforms: a cat's cradle of hummocks, some bald, others tufted with marram grass. Climbing to the top of a 10-metre-high crest at the centre of the mobile portion of the dune, Guignion said, "Try to think of this as a fresh meadow — that's what it was several years ago when we first came here to do bird surveys."

We had a full view of the Gulf of St. Lawrence, where the local lobster fleet was spread out between the beach and the horizon. Inland, a scrub zone of marram grass graded into distant bayberry bushes and wind-twisted white spruce, a natural plant succession that can occur in as few as 30 years in the process of dune stabilization.

Below us was Bog Pond, one of three large ponds interlaced with the dune. The combination of dune and wetland and the unusual productivity of St. Peters Bay led to a recommendation in 1974 that the area be declared an ecological reserve under the International Biological Programme.

Black ducks and teal worked the reedy shallows of Bog Pond. "These ponds are full of life. There's an incredible array of animals here," Guignion informed me, listing mink, fox, muskrat and raccoon. The diversity of wildlife has made the area a favourite haunt for generations of local trappers and hunters.

Guignion, a past president of the Island Nature Trust — a provincial organization dedicated to preserving the natural heritage of Prince Edward Island — doesn't find such traditional use incompatible with site preservation: "Part of the Trust's plan would include use by people, but at a level that wouldn't be detrimental to the plant and animal communities that are there. We feel traditional use is quite compatible with preservation as long as it is monitored."

Even though the dune has been designated as an environmental protection area, there is little actual protection. It is, on paper at least, private property, but people come and go at will. This practise has led to depredation of the dune, especially from the increased use of all-terrain cycles in recent years. I had seen two of the three-wheeled variety parked in a Greenwich Road yard.

After my firsthand inspection of the dune, I spoke with Dr. Ian MacQuarrie, a colleague of Guignion in the University of Prince Edward Island's biology department and the Island's foremost authority on dune biota. He compared the vulnerability of dunes to Arctic tundra, pointing to studies which have shown that just 10 people following a single course can cause damage for a whole season. Vehicle traffic can leave scars that remain visible for years. Scarring results from damage to the marram grass root system which forms a dense underground net binding the dune together. Once exposed, the root bundles are easily undermined by the wind. In dune terminology, a blowout occurs.

MacQuarrie feels that massive development like the Evans plan, cheek by jowl with an important wilderness area, constitutes "classic land-use conflict." Inevitably, he said, there would be a spillover of people from the residential complex and a destabilization of the dune. MacQuarrie emphasized the importance of reconciling environmental concerns with the very real human needs in the area.

Born on a small Island farm himself, and still a hobby farmer, MacQuarrie described his love of the land as "genetic." He elicited a heartfelt sympathy — admirable and surprising in one identified with the environmental movement — for the fate of St. Peters and Greenwich. "At one time," he said, "this was a very fine farming area. But because of the major changes that have happened, it's down to a handful of farmers. You've got a generation of people who have watched their children grow up and leave. They're quite bitter about it. To see a closely knit rural society falling apart like that is quite depressing. So I have trouble getting mad at people up there who support the development."

Despite its scenic attributes, St. Peters Bay has held to the old ways of Island life based on farming and fishing, eschewing the trappings of tourism that typify so much of the Island's north shore (notably at Stanhope and Cavendish). "It's frustrating for people at this end of the province," Aquinas Ryan, St. Peters' village chairman, told me. "They have been concerned with keeping the land in production, while other areas have opted for tourist development. Now they feel they've lost out."

There are still opportunities to make a working life in St. Peters Bay, but realizing them demands a versatile exploitation of all seasons and even the vicissitudes of weather. Norbert Palmer, who for me epitomizes the St. Peters Bay survivor, likened the local economy to a bag of jelly beans: "You like the black ones, the black ones are good; then perhaps you get sick of them, and you have to eat the red ones."

Lobsters are Palmers' mainstay. But he seines mackerel in late summer and fishes bluefin tuna that migrate into Gulf waters in the fall. He traps eels in the estuaries, and when a storm blows onshore, he collects Irish moss — a plant used in food and pharmaceutical manufacturing. North winds uproot the red seaweed from offshore rocks and bring it ashore at Cable Head, and then men, women and children flock to the beach in pickups for the harvest.

When there's "a fair shake of moss," as Palmer says, gatherers can earn a hundred dollars a day. "Some people might be at it for only one storm. The area is free, and if you have time you can go at it — if it suits you."

Palmer has recently added fox farming to his seasonal cycle, but his sanguine picture of personal freedom based on economic opportunism does not apply equally to all St. Peters Bay residents. For many, the bag of jelly beans is 10 weeks work, followed by 40 weeks of unemployment insurance. It is a pattern familiar to many Maritime rural communities.

The one expanding sector of the local economy, and the only alternative to tourism development, is mussel culture. St. Peters Bay has been famous for its mussel productivity since the 19th century, when farmers cut holes in ice and dredged the harbour bottom for "mussel mud." The grey beds of mussel shells were then spread on the fields as a limestone substitute. Today, strings of white buoys mark the area where clusters of mussels are suspended on plastic socks as they mature for market. But the future of the mussel industry, like most everything else I looked at in St. Peters Bay, depends on the uncertain fate of the Greenwich development.

One of those caught between the development and the growing mussel industry is Russel Dockendorf, a proud seventh generation Islander, the descendant of a British Empire Loyalist of German extraction. All of the Dockendorfs farmed until Russel's generation. "It came to the point where you had to mechanize, which meant a large expenditure, or you had to get out," he told me. Dockendorf chose the latter course, following a route taken by many Maritimers economically expatriated by the demise of the family farm. He worked in construction in Goose Bay, Labrador, then in Ontario.

In the end, his heart led him back to his Island home ("Ontario? I don't know," he reflected, "it's all right if you're born there, I guess"). He turned to the sea for his livelihood, and, today, he fishes for lobster and owns the St. Peters Bay mussel leases. Ironically, his business is now threatened by an influx of outsiders.

"If that went ahead and they got a marina and all that, it would be a real nuisance," he said. Dockendorf is a quiet man who gives the impression of wanting to avoid a controversy. A conflict is inevitable, however, if the development does proceed because the mussels are most productive in the deepest portions of the bay, the same areas best suited to boating. Dockendorf stands to lose half of this mussel-growing area. For now, the potential territorial dispute has been laid at the doorstep of the federal Department of Fisheries and Oceans.

Banking on government support for his position, Dockendorf recently invested in a mussel-processing facility for Greenwich. The expansion will double his full-time employees to 10 and will add an equal number of seasonal jobs. There is room for even more growth, but a 1981 environmental-impact assessment of the Greenwich development, the first ever commissioned by the provincial government, estimated that at best, the mussel industry could generate only 100 jobs; the dune development, on the other hand, might offer as many as 150. The service jobs would be seasonal and largely taken by women. They might provide a second income for families, summer jobs for local college students or a means for more young people to settle in St. Peters, rather than drift away to Charlottetown or off the Island entirely. As one civic-minded supporter of the development noted ironically: "We'll lose our identity unless we get some new blood."

Others worry, however, that a seasonal population will disrupt community integrity. "What I don't like," said Russel Dockendorf's son, Russel Jr., as we stood on the Red Head Wharf below the Dockendorf packing plant, looking across to the spring fields of Greenwich, "is the absolute distinction between the rich and the poor. You may find there's a fence at the entrance to Greenwich, and beyond that, you don't go unless you're going in to clean rooms."

I tried to imagine sails spangling the bay, golf carts scooting over the green fields and condominiums peeking out through manicured woods: an affluent daytime television community transplanted to a landscape shaped by the hard labour and frugality of descendants of highland Scots.

Already the Island has seen what would have been unimaginable a generation ago. Since 1950, two thirds of the working farms have disappeared, a trend accelerated in the last two decades by potato monomania and the currency of the bigger - is-better philosophy. These factors made the decline of Greenwich possible in the first place, according to David Weale, a University of Prince Edward Island history professor who is writing a history of Island farming.

"The philosophy of the time was the small farmer couldn't make it. So when hotshots like Evans came along, they sold out."

Weale served as secretary to Premier Angus MacLean, a blueberry farmer who promised, but couldn't deliver, a "rural renaissance" during a two year tenure of power ending in 1981. Still, Weale holds on to the slim hope that the small Island farm will make a comeback and, with it, communities like Greenwich. "It might be a bit visionary," he admitted, "but I like to think the land can still provide a living for more, rather than fewer, people."

It does seem a vision born more of wishful thinking than of any pragmatic scrutiny of reality. There are now only two working farms on the Greenwich Road, where two decades ago, the local creamery truck made stops at 20 farm gates twice a week.

One of the extant farms belongs to Robert Rossiter. While not the typical century-farm bed and breakfast type property, it is still pleasantly bucolic. Ayrshires grazed in the pasture beside the long farm lane leading to a new bungalow and a steel-sided barn. I chatted with Mary Rossiter about the Greenwich development as she unpacked groceries from her weekly shopping trip to the Co-op, the last of the three general stores that St. Peters once supported.

"I think it would be nice," she said. "St. Peters will be a ghost town in a couple of years. Most of the people are already senior citizens, and I think, my God, we really need something. What is around for the young people unless you farm or fish or get a little job at the store? There's nothing for them here. And it's not like it's going to be a casino, like a lot of people have been claiming. If it's going to keep people in the community and add some jobs, I can't see a thing wrong with it."

Though some Greenwich households are divided on the issue, the Rossiters' is not. When Robert joined us in the kitchen, he was emphatic." I look at it this way: You can't have your cake and eat it too. I've got four kids; you can't just think of yourself." He doesn't give credence to the idea that the development conflicts with farming. The bushes growing up on the Land Development Corporation fields along the Greenwich Road are there, he said, simply because local farmers no longer want to farm them.

I drove on toward Hubert Sanderson's farm, the unpurchased link in the chain of properties that Evans needs in order to proceed with the development.

"It used to be a great farming section," Sanderson declared, setting two steaming cups of tea on the kitchen table, "but since the neighbouring farms have been sold, you really got nobody to go to for a helping hand. There used to be three of us here who worked together. To me, it's changed here — quite a change." A heaviness settled in his throat.

Sanderson has always maintained that he wouldn't stand in the way of development, only that he wanted a fair price for the farm in which he has invested 33 years of labour. If Evans does not buy his farm, Sanderson doubts whether any other farmer would be interested in it now, because the character of the community has been so altered. "I was too late in selling the place, and I guess that's why I'm stuck here yet," he said.

Our talk turned to the dune, and Sanderson warmed to the memories of his childhood. In those days, he said, the foredunes were 100 feet high, and he and his brothers would dangle over the edge trying to catch cliff swallows. Catastrophic winter storms toppled them in the 1930's. He remembered the old Acadian burial ground at the mouth of the bay, the chapel cellar where he and his father rid the farm of fieldstone and two 20-acre fields, long-lost features of the land that were, as he said, "all sanded over now."

He also remembered an axe that Leith Sanderson had stuck in a stump when a winter storm drove him home from the wood grove that stood where the dune is now. It was not until 35 years later that the rusted axe head and the rotten stub of the handle were found. The inexorable movement of the sand exposed it, just as it had buried it more than three-decades earlier.

Sanderson's story of the buried axe struck me as having a lot in common with the Greenwich development. Since the proposal first surfaced two decades ago, it has exhibited a capacity for going underground, then resurfacing unexpectedly.

Greenwich has become a powerful and persistent symbol of the loving care that Islanders hold for the land — a care lyrically expressed by the late Island laureate Milton Acorn: " Nowhere that plowcut worms heal themselves in red loam; spruces squat, skirts in sand or the stones of a river rattle its dark tunnel under the elms is there a spot not measured by hands."

Regardless of the outcome of the Greenwich controversy, its tortuous history will stand as a testament of the Islanders' deeply rooted attachment to the land — their tie that binds.

III. DIEHARD PRIDE

For a time in the late 1970s, I lived in the coaltown of River Hebert in Cumberland County. While there I gained an insight not only into the workings of a mine but the culture of mining. Minetowns have a kind of diehard pride in the specialized function they perform, though they receive little thanks for it from an outside world that cannot understand why men subject themselves to the rigour and dangers of mining and even less why many prefer it to any other kind of work.

Nova Scotians owe coalminers a great debt, for it was coal from Cape Breton Island, and Pictou and Cumberland Counties, that fueled our factories and heated our homes until very recently. I have already spoken of the appalling conditions endured by the miners of River Hebert. In a sense they were the lucky ones for not far away, in the deeper, higher, more modern mines of Springhill, men — too many men — lost their lives. No one alive in the 1950s can forget the two mine disasters, and in particular the infamous Bump of 1958 that finally brought mining to a tragic conclusion in Springhill. The new technique of on-site television reporting seared the drama of Springhill into the collective unconscious of North Americans, so that the very name has entered the lexicon as a synonym of heroism and tragedy. It is fitting that none of us forget the Springhill experience. A quarter century after the Bump I returned to the town on the hill to find out what Springhillers themselves remembered, to turn over the coals of memory, which still smolder there like the inextinguishable underground fires in the old mine workings under the town.

These two stories are not merely reminders of a way of life relegated permanently to a distant past. In Cape Breton 2,400 men still travel several kilometers under the ground, tunneling out under the sea, to dig out the coal that turns on our lights in a province where much of the power is coal-generated. We cannot yet forget, as many might prefer, that men daily risk their lives and health in mines so that we can continue our comfortable lives above ground — in the light.

MINING A THIN SEAM WASN'T GOD'S IDEA

The bankhead rears up like a colossal, black-boned skeleton exhumed from the tidal mud. It looks so rickety, I question last night's decision to defer a life-insurance option. Even Ron Beaton, owner of the coal mine in River Hebert, N.S., says, "It's a relic." It's the last unmechanized thin-seam mine in the province and, in it, 100 men daily hack out coal, as their grandfathers did. River Hebert has mined coal for 130 years and, in the 1930's, 19 men died here in explosions. Successive provincial governments have subsidized Beaton's mine to protect jobs. But last spring, dangerous gas levels revived old rumours that the mine would shut down forever, and mine officials give it two years at best. Meanwhile, the men keep going down. Most are under 30; some have no skills to sell, just their youth and strength.

Underground manager Ralph Henwood accompanies me on the tour and, as we board an empty coal car, a light mist billows from the slope's black mouth. I lie propped on an elbow, heeding Ralph's warning to keep my head down. The spring sun vanishes behind us. Ralph shouts above the rumbling track: "This mine takes you back to the turn of the century. In Springhill, the slope was arched with concrete." My lamp scans the hardwood pit props. Water spits on us from sagging, cobweb-festooned roof supports. It takes only a couple of minutes to travel through the millennia of geological years to the first level: 2,500 feet underground. Disembarking from the coal car, I stoop to avoid striking my head on the slant roof, and a rat scurries down the dark tunnel ahead of me.

A few hundred feet in from the slope, Ralph stops to check for methane with his meter. Water and poor roof conditions have also plagued the miners, and the word is that the men are into "bad ground." Now a concussion recoils from deep in the mine's bowels. The rock walls, roof and floor shudder, and "BUMP" whiplashes

69

into my mind. Smoke sucks past me, as adrenalin flushes my veins. But Ralph reads my look of alarm and gently advises, "They're blasting at the coal face."

Pandemonium greets us at the face: Curses and barked instructions compete with the deafening rhythm of the shaker pan. Miners' lamps cut through the dust and smoke. My mind and gut tighten to accommodate the claustrophobic dimension that is the men's working space. Miners kneel, or lie on their sides and backs, to shovel their bed of coal into the pan. They have no choice. The wall is only 33 inches deep and pitches at a sharp angle. An older miner snarls about the position in which someone on the night shift has left the cutter (a big chain that undercuts the seam). Irritably, he prods the roof with his pick. " And this roof isn't too goddamned good either."

"The roof is slate," Ralph tells me. "That's what makes it dangerous. A sandstone roof is much more stable."

Squirming under the roof, I flip onto my back and, to ease myself down the grade, dig in heels and elbows. In places, there's barely room to fit myself between the "packs" of hardwood timber that buttress the roof. Rows of packs recede into the dim distance where the coal has been extracted. The weight between the face and the main slope has squashed some to a fraction of their original height. Where the roof takes on weight near the wall, men keep wedging in more timber. Still, it is as if each miner were an Atlas, bearing his slate-skied heaven on his own shoulders and knees. Every eight or nine days lately, the roof has been "taking a set"; with a thunderous warning, the stone above squeezes your crawl-space closer to extinction.

When we reach the lower level, I regain my feet. "That's a weight off your shoulders" has never had more meaning. And at the top of the slope the light of spring has never been more welcome. At noon the men stretch out on the narrow benches in the lunch room. Ribbing soon gives way to stoic talk: of the Glace Bay miner who died last night in hospital; of the first anniversary of Hector McKeigan's death at River Hebert. "Carelessness causes most mining accidents," one miner says. "It's always the good roof that kills people." I reflect that there may never be another pit like the one these men know, and perhaps that's just as well. As one man who spent 52 years in River Hebert-Joggins mines told me: "I don't think God ever intended Man to mine a thin seam."

AFTER THE BUMP

The dignitaries are standing with military attentiveness against the sun-blasted stucco of the Miners' Hall, an elongated structure crowned with a cupola. Wooden racks that will soon be filled with memorial wreaths have been propped up on either side of the monuments. A loose crowd has assembled on the street. Women and children are perched on a retaining wall; a clutch of old men rally around a telephone pole.

"Great day to be going down No. 2," one offers.

"I've been down better," the other replies, dismissively.

The hushed conversations are abruptly curtailed by the dropping of a needle onto a well-used recording of *O Canada*.

It is the kind of ceremony that is repeated in towns and cities across Canada. But this act of remembrance is not taking place under the leaden ceiling of a November sky. It's June, and the cenotaph is across the street. The memorial that commands attention is a white sandstone figure, a mustachioed miner who has overlooked Main Street in Springhill, Nova Scotia, for nearly a century. His pedestal bears 125 names. At the base, 39 names are engraved on a footstone, and a few feet to his right is a headstone with yet another 75 names chiselled into its granite face. Each name represents a man or boy who was lowered into the coal-rich depths under this town of 5,225 citizens only to be hoisted to the surface crushed, battered or burned by the explosions of 1891 and 1956 and, finally, by the 1958 Bump that put an end to big-time mining in this hilltop town.

The town's courageous struggle for survival in the late 1950's engaged the sympathy of the world. This day, 100 Springhillers are quietly remembering their own — spared the fickle attention of the media's interlopers. They are honouring not only the men who died in the headline-making disasters but all 424 men who have lost their lives in Springhill mines, the majority in the day-to-day accidents that are a grim fact of life in any mining town.

In *Blood on the Coal: The Story of the Springhill Mining Disasters*, Roger David Brown writes that Springhill was first settled in 1790 by three Empire Loyalists. Originally, coal was mined from outcrops — surface deposits — and sold to blacksmiths. Commercial mining began in 1849. By 1891, when the first and most tragic of the disasters struck, there were 1,350 males working in three Springhill mines. Many were boys, who performed the menial, but back-breaking, tasks.

At 12:43 p.m., February 21, 1891, a massive explosion ripped through the mine, the result of a slippage of stone that allowed flame from a routine blasting operation to escape into the gassy, dust-filled workings. "The explosion at Springhill was different from the two other major mine disasters the town was to endure," Brown writes. "After 2 o'clock, a little over an hour after the explosion, no survivors came out of the mine. There was no miracle."

On November 1, 1956, another explosion rocked Springhill. A seven-car train loaded with coal had become unhooked and gone on a wild careering rampage through the haulage slope of the No. 4 mine. At the 4,400-foot level (the depth of a mine is measured on the slope, not in vertical feet), it jumped the track and crushed a 2,200-volt cable. A wall of flame roared to the surface and shot 200 feet into the cold November sky. Three walls of the bank head collapsed, and people came running to the foot of Main Street, many to help in the rescue effort, others to stand helplessly by, waiting. For some, the wait was not in vain. Although 39 men died, 88 others emerged from the mine's depths. One group of 47 survived for three and a half days in the gas-filled mine by notching a compressed air hose that remained intact, then breathing its life-giving oxygen.

Although two of Springhill's major disasters were caused by explosions, the most ominous characteristic of the Springhill mines was their tendency to "bump." In the 40 years prior to 1958, more than 500 bumps had been recorded in the No. 2 mine.

Simply defined, a bump is a rock burst, a sudden failure of the coal seam brought on by excessive stress. The coal itself is violently expelled into the working area, and in major bumps, the floor heaves, crushing everything in its wake.

Restricted to relatively few mining areas in the world, bumping always occurs in association with a strong roof stratum, such as the hard sandstone that overlies the Springhill coal seams. In long-wall mining, as practised in Springhill, the miners' safety —

strange as it may sound — depended upon the roof collapsing behind them, in the waste area, as the seam of coal was extracted, thus allowing for a gradual release of pressure. The strong sandstone roof resisted caving in, however, and as more coal was extracted, this solid beam of rock acted as a cantilever, putting more and more pressure on the coal face, until it burst, or bumped, in colliers' terms.

In 1958, the No. 2 mine, which had been worked continuously since 1873, was the only mine left in Springhill. It was also the deepest coal mine in the world, having been mined to a vertical depth of 4,340 feet. Bumping had begun to occur at the 2,000-foot level, and the frequency had increased with depth. Most were mild pressure bumps that nevertheless accounted for more than 100 fatalities. Every Springhill miner knew that a major shock bump was coming; he just hoped that it wasn't on his shift.

The tremor was registered at 8:06 p.m., October 23, 1958, on seismographs in Sept Isle, Quebec, and in Ottawa. Seventy-five men lost their lives. But after six and a half days, and the near abandonment of hope by rescue workers, a group of 12 men were found alive. Two days later, another group of six were disinterred from their living grave. They had been eating coal and bark, and in the final days, they were forced to drink their own urine in order to survive.

The relatively new medium of television kept a constant vigil over the unfolding drama, and reporters dispatched their stories to newspapers across the continent. The miners' ordeal became a parable of human endurance, and Springhill itself entered the lexicon of the North American collective unconscious. Springhill still seems to occupy a paranoiac dark pocket of the mind, a place where a fear of the earth suddenly collapsing under you is palpable.

The durability of the town's hardluck image naturally displeases many Springhillers. Except for the ritualistic observance of the town's tragic history, many would just as soon forget the three dates commemorated on Monument Hill. That is particularly true for the men who actually survived the disasters.

Hugh Guthro was trapped in both modern disasters: for two and a half days at the 4,400-foot level in 1956 and for six days at the 13,000-foot level in 1958. I almost expect someone of heroic stature, but Guthro is a small, wiry man — an advantage in low-roofed mines. He sits at the kitchen table, cupping the knee of his drawn-up right leg in both hands, a compact posture that he no doubt often assumed in the mines.

He talks freely: "I know one night, I nearly choked the daylights out of the wife." He demonstrates, crooking his arm like a wrestler applying a headlock. "You know, something happened in the mine that night, and I pretty near choked her to death. I was saying, 'Get down, get down, the roof's coming in.' Christ, she would tell me about it in the morning, and I wouldn't remember doing it. But this was after the Bump and that...but that was 25 years ago. I don't think too much about what really did happen, now."

In the aftermath of the 1958 Bump, Guthro, like many Springhill miners, was forced to leave his hometown to find work. He went to Labrador to work for the Iron Ore Company of Canada. But in 1960, when the Syndicate Mine opened, he was back digging coal in Springhill. When it closed in 1970, he moved to the River Hebert Mine, 20 miles away.

He thought nothing of returning to the mines, despite being buried alive twice. Like most miners, he is philosophical about the dangers. "This was a way of life, and this is the way everybody worked here." And he was proud: He preferred mining to unemployment. Today, however, he is happy with his job at the Surrette Battery factory. A mine is the furthest thing from his mind. "I'm 55 years old. You start thinking. Well, when you get this far in life, you don't want to go back into a mine."

Today, if you drive into Springhill from the New Brunswick border, the first intersection brings you hard up against the town's mining past. The Miners' Hall and monuments stand at the top of Main Street. Facing the hall are two rather large wooden churches; opposite, there is a Lucky Dollar store. It has seen better days. The asphalt-grey siding covers a false western storefront; attached is a boarded-up warehouse. Proprietor Fraser Mills produces a bottle of pop from the walk-in meat cooler, claiming that it is the coldest in town — an honest boast. I learn that it is a family business, and I ask what effect the mine closing had on merchants.

"Since the war, really," he offers, "we all knew something violent was going to happen, and of course, it did. But that pretty much was the low point. After that, it had to get better."

Fires have left a visible mark on Springhill — even more than the mines have. Driving down the steep serpentine incline of Main Street, I was struck first by its incompleteness, then by a lack of

74

architectural continuity. A fire in 1957 levelled much of the upper half of Main Street; another in 1975 took up where the first left off, destroying 18 buildings in the lower half — leaving the town without a commercial district to speak of.

The rebuilding process has been painfully slow. There is a new Stedman's, a modern split-level municipal building and a Bank of Commerce, which probably had something to do with the benevolence of the bank's prime-time attraction, singer Anne Murray. A large blow-up poster of Springhill's most famous daughter, framed in a Nova Scotian tartan border, hangs on the municipal building's brick facade. "Welcome to Our County" captions a girl-next-door image of Murray.

Springhillers are proud of the international acclaim accorded the smoky-voiced daughter of a local doctor. They are also grateful for the face of success that Murray has helped put on the "hard-luck town" — the media's cliche of convenience since the 1950's. For many, that epithet has been a matter of personal shame. A Springhill resident describes her first trip as a teenager away from her hometown: "When you told people you were from Springhill, they looked at you as if you had some kind of disease — that was before Anne Murray made it."

A few wooden stores that remained intact at the lower end of Main Street emanate a kind of fusty charm. Lorne Smith, 37, runs a lunch counter at the front of one of the town's oldest businesses, the Springhill Candy Kitchens. A vinyl stool at the black arborite counter was as good a place as any to get an inkling of the town's feisty spirit.

Smith does not so much serve his customers as taunt them into good-humoured acceptance of what he's handing out: fries, burgers and a good ribbing to boot.

"Since you're hanging around doing nothing, you want to pick up that waste? And try not to limp."

It is the type of repartee that one almost expects to find in a mining town where poking fun was developed to a high degree. Smith was obviously a good student. He is one of many Springhillers who came back to his hometown after a decade away. Pressed for his personal reasons, he replies, "I had a young family then, and I wanted them to grow up seeing the same things I did."

Things have changed considerably, however, since Smith was a kid in the 1950's. There are no longer two hotels and six menswear shops. Now, there isn't even a theatre for a children's Saturday matinee.

Smith attempted to revive his father's clothing business, but the venture ended in bankruptcy. He accepts most of the blame, but he also discovered that after the fires, customers had gotten into the habit of shopping in the shire town of Amherst, 15 miles northwest of Springhill.

"You can't think with your heart. You got to think with your head," Smith says, unconvincingly. He is a bit like the town itself: heart-strong, proud, tenacious and more than a little philosophical — tragedy teaches you that if you're going to survive. "The trauma people went through, you won't find that any place else. In that sense, this town is *great*," he concludes emphatically, just to be sure that I don't go away with the wrong impression.

The spirit that prevailed over the succession of disasters in the 1950s has had to carry on in the face of chronic economic ills. Mayor William Mont contends, with justification, that economically, Springhill is only 25 years old. There was no phase-out period: One day, 1,400 men went to work; the mine bumped; and that night, it was all over.

The town has converted the old mine grounds at the base of Main Street into an industrial park. The mine buildings are now occupied by small manufacturers of plastics, batteries and furnaces. They have proved themselves reliable employers — even during the recent recession. But the mainstay of Springhill is the federal medium-security institution located on the outskirts of town. Over a beer at the Lamp Cabin Tavern, a guard tells me: "It used to be the pit, now it's the joint."

The prison provides far fewer jobs (350) than the mines did at their peak. But the $20,000-plus institutional salaries have given Springhill a surer economic base than the mines were able to in their last days, plagued as they were by frequent shutdowns.

Economically inconstant, the mines were, nevertheless, a unifying force for the community — something the prison will never be. If for that reason only, many Springhillers lament their passing. "Any coal-mining town has a very strong esprit de corps among the population," Mont explains. (Mont worked in the mine's machine shop but is now a prison employee.)

"It just made for a family type of attitude, or feeling, with the townspeople — but that's slowly disappearing. As you get people

76

who never worked in the mines, and their fathers are dying off, and they don't know anything about the coal-mining era, it'll be like any other town."

To understand the character of a coal-mining town, it is necessary to know something about what takes place in the cramped workings that spread under it like a subterranean maze. It is there that loyalties and interdependencies which bind the community into a hermetic whole are forged.

In a one-industry town like Springhill, mining was an economic imperative. "You see, that's the way it was when we was growing up," a former miner says. "We just followed down in the footsteps." But given the choice, most miners would take the pit over any other workplace. The explanation most often given for this mystifying attachment is, "Mining gets into the blood."

Harry Munroe is a direct descendant of Henry Swift, the underground manager at the time of the 1891 explosion. All of his people were miners. It was the romance of the miners' oral tradition that first attracted him to the mines as a boy: "I used to be fascinated to hear them talking about the mines. I couldn't wait to get down into a mine and see what it was like — they never pictured it as a place you wouldn't like."

Now 55, Munroe, like many other Springhill boys, went into the mines as soon as he could, at the age of 16. The realities of life underground didn't disillusion him: "There was never two days the same in the mine. It was like every day was a challenge."

"And of course," Munroe continues, taking visible pleasure in his subject, "the thing, too, was that the miners themselves were like a breed of people who are separate. I don't know where you'd ever find people like them. They made their own entertainment. Maybe this was one of the ways of shedding fear...it was the sense of humour that took away the drab of the job."

Men actually went to work hours early to pick up on a yarn that had been spun out the day before. The company provided a place, known as the Pest House, for just that purpose. Today, old miners carry on the tradition in the basement of the Miners' Hall, on the steps of the federal building or on several sidewalk "liars' benches."

This camaraderie found its practical expression in the buddy system. For reasons of safety, miners always worked in pairs. Ultimately, their interdependence was couched in the sacred miners' code: in case of disaster, miners on the surface would work

77

without rest until the last living man, or the last body, was found. Munroe actually ended his mining career as a Draegerman, carrying out that grim charge after the Bump.

Dominion Steel and Coal Corporation (DOSCO) sealed off the entrance to the No. 2 mine in July 1959. Although DOSCO had operated the Springhill mines since 1913, no provision had been made for the fate that awaits all mining towns — someday, the mines shut down for good. "I know fellows that worked 47 years who didn't get a cent," recalls the United Mine Workers' last local secretary, Cecil Colwell. "When No. 2 bumped and didn't reopen, all these men were never offered a pension. At the time, there were no pension funds at all."

Money poured into the Springhill Disaster Relief Fund from all over the world, eventually swelling it to $2 million. But that only compensated the widows and the very needy men who were either disabled by the disaster or too old to find alternative employment. They received $40 a week. Many men, who had known nothing but the mines, simply had to pack their bags and leave. Springhill's population shrank from more than 7,000 to less than 5,000.

The corollary of "Mining gets into the blood" is "Mining towns die hard." Although large-scale mining was brought to an abrupt halt by the Bump, mining has never entirely stopped in Springhill. Immediately after the closing of No. 2, illegal bootleg mines sprang up wherever there was an outcrop of a few accessible tons of coal in old workings. The last bootleg mine was closed in 1981, causing a furore in the local press.

Currently, there is a controversial strip mine on the outskirts of town, the planned first phase of an underground mine. A political decision is pending on whether to press ahead with the second phase. The surface (or strip) method of mining flies in the face of a century of mining tradition in Springhill. To Springhillers, a mine must go underground to be considered a mine. If you broach the subject of the strip mine with the former miners who meet everyday "overtown," on the steps of the federal building (a sort of open-air Pest House), you may get a shrug and a guttural dismissal of your loose use of language. If they discuss it at all, it is as a conundrum and an irritation. "I don't see what kind of mine they're supposed to be startin' out there."

Mary Raper was attending night school when her class was interrupted by a dreadful bang. As she ran from the school, she

78

asked the janitor if a car had hit the building. "No," he answered. She knew better than to ask, for her husband had been telling her for months that there was going to be one big bump and that nobody would come out alive. Some did, but not John Raper.

"It was six days before they got my husband. It was just pure hell," Mary recalls from the living room of the two-storey home that her husband built. On this quiet, well-kept side street, whose entire length is visible from Mary's living-room window, 11 other families lost a father, a husband or a brother. There wasn't a Springhill home unmarked by the 1958 disaster.

For Mary, it was not the first bitter encounter with the tragedy that so often envelops mining towns. Her father, who was a miner in Durham, England, was killed when she was 16. "It just seems to go right through," she says, sadness clinging to her broad accent. "Thank God, my children won't be killed in the mine." It is a sentiment that many Springhill widows share.

It is unlikely that there will ever be another major tragedy in a Springhill mine, as provincial regulations now prevent mining at a depth below 2,000 feet, where serious bumping began to occur. But a question that gets its due in the sidewalk congresses is whether 100 or 200 men will be found to work the new mine — especially young men.

Guy Brown, the local Liberal Member of the Legislative Assembly, supports a small mine, but only for the men put of work by the closing of the Syndicate and River Hebert Mines. He is adamant that a mine is not a long-term solution for the town's young people: "Let's not take our young people who are 19 and 20 and put them into the ground if they know the thing will close in 15 or 20 years."

Old miners seem loath to accept that ineluctable fact. The rhythm of the mines — the mechanical underground cacophony and the esprit de corps which manifested itself in the human ebb and flow between shifts — is the pulse that still controls their passions. It runs deeply and richly through their beings. They cling tenaciously to the notion that the only thing which will ever do Springhill any good is another coal mine.

Even if the new mine gets the green light, the way of life in Springhill will never again be dictated by the advance of a 400-foot-long wall of coal. Those days are gone forever. But remembering Springhill the way it was remains important — not just to those who lived it. It is more than a nostalgic exercise or old men clinging stubbornly to the romanticism of mining.

In *The Road to Wigan Pier*, published in the 1930s, George Orwell wrote: "Our civilization is founded on coal....In the metabolism of the western world, the coal miner is second in importance only to the man who ploughs the soil. He is sort of a grimy caryatid upon whose shoulders everything *not* grimy is supported." On the eve of 1984, Orwell's observation about civilization's dependency on coal is no longer true. But as a description of a way station in civilization's advance, it remains valid. And for the world of the mining town, that utter dependency on coal is always valid until there is no more or until the price paid for extracting it is too great in either economic or human terms. This was Springhill's fate.

In Springhill, men followed the seams of coal deeper and deeper into the earth, beyond the point where the coal could be hoisted to the surface at a profit and, tragically, beyond the point where the coal could support the mass of earth above it. It was as if society had forgotten why these men went into the underworld every day, following rhythms we no longer understood or even cared about, until the world caved in under their little town. Then we focused our attention on every detail of their dark lives, with a blinding and sometimes cruel intensity. We witnessed their courage and endurance and extracted what moral lesson we could from the heart-rending drama. It is a lesson worth remembering, especially as the consumer society scrambles to satisfy its materialism and as coal once again becomes an acceptable energy source.

I stood in the June sun, trying to pay respect to the men who climbed into the man-rake, never to see the light of day again. But I got closer to them at the Springhill Miners' Museum.

Retired miners lead you through the washhouse, where clothes are hung from the ceiling (like effigies) by ropes and pulleys, as if the shift were going to return, don them and head for home. Finally, they guide you to the black mouth of a mine tunnel. You awkwardly descend the 30-degree slope. Three hundred feet down, you strike coal. Children and adults can try their hands at picking some — it is harder than you imagine.

Then without notice, the electric lights are momentarily doused. Your breath catches in a fleeting second of remembrance in the absolute darkness — blacker than coal or night.

IV. TO THE WOODS

Maritimers and Newfoundlanders have always gone to "the woods" — to cut pulp and firewood, to hunt, or simply to escape the fields and the sea where they made a living. In the past people treated the woods with respect for it satisfied a number of needs, economic and aesthetic, and therefore had to be tended with an eye to the future. I think there has always been a strong emotional attachment to the woods simply because that's all that was given in the beginning. The woods were the stake for our ancestors. And what they made of it is what we have today.

Now the woods stand at our backs whispering accusations. In their beleaguered state they seem to pass judgement on our stewardship. Gone are the "vast cathedrals" the first settlers ecstatically described. They went away in the planks, masts and holds of the sailing ships which were the agents of the region's brief Golden Age.

But there were still a few virgin stands of trees when Murray Prest was a boy growing up in Mooseland, Nova Scotia. They made a lasting impression on him, and ever since Prest has fought a battle to retain what is best in the forest through sound management learned at the knee of an earlier generation of homegrown foresters. To his dismay, this native expertise was ignored when, in the mid-1960s, the Nova Scotia government gave away public forest lands to foreign interests in exchange for a few industrial wages in a pulp and paper mill. It seems that we got much more than we bargained for, as destruction of the forest has since accelerated at an unprecedented rate.

We hear a great deal today about the global economy. Often the phrase engenders a feeling of helplessness; we seem to have lost control of our own destiny to faceless external forces, which, we are told, are shaping our lives and futures.

I have found that the problem is often rooted closer to home. In fact, we have forfeited control because we have been unwilling to assume responsibility for the management of our own resources — in particular the forest. As a result, in a Kafkaesque turn of events, people end up fighting their own politicians, the very people they have entrusted to protect the common interest.

Perhaps nowhere has this battle between individuals and the apparatus of government been more protracted and concerted than in New Brunswick, where for forty years concerned citizens have waged a campaign against the chemical management of their forests.

Maritimers are not known for their vocal opposition to authority. In the past they have accepted the credo expressed by the pulpcutter father of poet Alden Nowlan: "You keep your mouth shut and your ass close to the ground." Good advice, I suppose, when a spray plane is buzzing your property and dumping hundreds of gallons of toxic chemicals on your head.

It fell to women to rise up against a programme that in the name of protecting the forest endangered the lives of their children. They were reviled for their courage. "We're always accused of being emotional," Catherine Richards of the Concerned Parents group told me. "I think it's because we called ourselves 'parents' and a lot of us were women so that the label was an easy one to apply."

Parents might be forgiven for being emotional when they have good reason to believe that their child has died of Reye's syndrome as a result of exposure to a spruce budworm spray. It is harder to forgive the rationalizations of government, epitomized in a notorious statement by New Brunswick's Minister of Natural Resources in 1976: "I don't like to see people dying. This is one of the things I really wouldn't like to see. But at the same time, knowing the forest as it is, my decision will have to be with the forest and the future of New Brunswick."

"The Enemy Above" (which won a national award for Public Affairs reporting) brought upon my head a shower of poisonous invective. One industry spokesman vented his spleen by calling me "a snake" and identifying me as a member of a subculture, "the radical-lib left," that I had never heard of, before or since. If anything, my journalistic pursuits have taught me that I am very much a product of my rural environment — and that my longheld conservationist's view arose directly and naturally from my early experience in the backwoods.

PREST'S LAST STAND

The tail of his L.L. Bean shirt flying, Murray Prest strides through the woods with the fierce energy of a man charged with an urgent mission. Occasionally, he stops to cast a wary eye over the carpet of spruce needles. He points out the stumps of yellow birch that are now reduced to rich reddish mounds of mulch camouflaged with a moss cap — fertilizer for the forest floor. At the base of a tall, straight red spruce, he kneels to note that the squirrels have been scattering the seed, a sign of the tree's reproductive maturity. He spies and clutches a mat of moss that is the pedestal for a red spruce seedling no larger than the size of his thumb, gently overturns the clod to determine whether the young tree has established a secondary root system. Satisfied that it has, he replaces it, then moves on up the hill, contemptuously brushing past a dead balsam fir pole that has been choked out by the faster growing overstory of red spruce. "Nature's way of spacing red spruce," is all Prest can muster by way of a compliment for the undistinguished fir.

It has been 30 years since Prest selectively cut over this ground, working the hardwood hills for the yellow birch — "Then, you could go to hell and back for a good hardwood tree, it was worth something" — and taking the mature red spruce for sawlogs. But he took care to leave the young spruce to mature, thinking that he would be back to harvest them when they had produced a seed crop for a future generation.

This time-proven forest practice was typical in Nova Scotia when Prest began working in the woods in the 1950's. Even as a boy, he learned the practical and moral principles of good forestry by watching the Eastern Shore woodsmen.

"I remember them working a crosscut saw in between trees, and if there was a little tree standing there, they would say, 'Don't cut that one down, that's one for the young fellas.' I mean, there's no such thing as that kind of care or concern for the forest today.

"We're destroying our forest, we're mining it, and we're destroying it as fast as we can," he says, bracing himself against a sturdy spruce. " Now, if I could just see that level off.... I'd be happy if I could see that indication."

Murray Prest has lived all of his 58 years in the tiny village of Mooseland. It is tucked into the forested interior of Nova Scotia, midway between the pastoral elm-lined Musquodoboit River Valley and the Eastern Shore, a rocky, sparsely populated stretch of coast between Halifax and Cape Breton Island. Surrounded by rivers, lakes and bogs and underlaid with granite and the merest dusting of topsoil where the glacier left any at all, it took a gold strike to put it on the map in 1858. That's when the first Prest came to Mooseland seeking his fortune, 100 years after his ancestor had been given a land grant on the Eastern Shore as separation pay from the British Army.

Mooseland's gold rush days lasted until the early 1900's. Then people turned to the rich resources of the woods. There were virgin stands of the unusually diverse and productive mix that characterizes the Acadian Forest: red spruce, yellow birch, hemlock, white pine and rock maple. Mooseland's water-powered mills turned out everything from molasses puncheons (80-gallon casks) for the West Indies to hardwood tongue depressors. Log drives down the Tangier River fed Canada's first sulphite pulp mill at nearby Sheet Harbour. Even during the depths of the Great Depression, there was no lack of work in Mooseland.

In 1946, when Murray Prest returned home from active duty as an Air Force gunner, there were five mills. Everyone expected the war to be followed by another depression, so timberland was going dirt cheap. The young entrepreneur, only 21, saw his opportunity, bought up land and opened his own mill. He quickly established markets for his quality hardwood and softwood in New England, the Caribbean and overseas. Eventually, his five younger brothers joined the booming family business.

Today, an unnatural calm hangs over Mooseland and the Prest Brothers Mill. A "No Trespassing" sign warns visitors off the empty lumberyard. Across the way, the schoolyard, too, is empty. The mill sports a new coat of grey paint, but its serviceable exterior is deceptive. Inside, there is only a hollow silence. The saws and planers long ago went to the auction block. It has been nearly a decade since the resinous smell of newly sawn lumber or the high pitched wail of a saw charged the Mooseland air.

Mooseland, which survived so long because of the woods, is now caught where it is — for a while longer, anyway — in spite of the woods. It is an intriguing and supreme irony that is certainly not lost on Murray Prest: "We're right in the middle of the woods. We should have been able to carry on forever," he notes in his disarmingly unguarded way.

Premature retirement does not suit Murray Prest. His brisk movements belie the kind of physical energy that abhors being penned up in the house. His face has the ruddy hue of the out-doorsman; in fact, he spends a good deal of his time in the woods, cruising his lands, hunting and fishing. But he has also dedicated long hours to the study of the evolution — or devolution — of Nova Scotia's forests and forest policy, to which his amassed files, clippings and correspondence bear witness. He has put together a damning case of abdication of political responsibility.

"It's just fantastic that you could take an inventory, a fabulous amount of wealth, and you could squander it, to destroy so many jobs and the livelihood of so many people, and end up with nothing."

Prest is one of the victims but feels that he got off easily. The big losers, he contends, are the forest itself and the future generations that would have profited from proper management. Prest's personal troubles began in the early 1960's. He had private holdings of 14,000 acres, but selective cutting had depleted his reserves of mature sawlogs to the point that he could not keep up with demand. He refused to cut immature stands — "You don't cut tomorrow's crop, it's not good business" — so that he was obliged to lease Crown land and to buy stumpage from Scott Paper, which had large freeholdings of its own in the area. For a few years, it proved a workable and amicable arrangement for all parties: "We cut the mature stuff and paid them for it, and everybody seemed to be happy."

However, Prest, like other lumbermen in the province, could not have foreseen the dramatic shift in government policy that took place in 1965, with the signing of the Scott Maritime Pulp Limited Agreement Act. Nova Scotia lumbermen bitterly resent the Act to this day, believing that it bargained their birthright with the giveaway of Crown land to the multinational corporation. It seemed to the lumbermen that their own government was turning its back on homegrown industry to please outsiders. The sense of betrayal cut deep.

The Scott Act was the welcome mat laid out for the Philadelphia-based multinational forestry giant by the new government of Premier Robert Stanfield. The benefits included a 20-year tax break on all forest land owned by or leased to the company as well as on the site of its new pulp mill at Abercrombie Point, Pictou County. The federal government contributed $5 million and an additional five-year income tax holiday. The 230,000 acres in eastern Halifax County that Nova Scotia leased to Scott Maritime had some of the finest standing timber left in the province. And critically, for Prest, it was this very land that he had been leasing from the government and which he was counting on for a future assured source of sawlogs.

"We were kind of having a love affair with industry at any cost," explains Prest. "That's when we started looking for whatever we could give away to buy industry. The forest was one of the things".

Although the Scott takeover of the Crown land leases was a major factor in the eventual demise of Prest's mill, his lasting resentment toward government relates to its abandonment of protective legislation for the forest.

The same day that the Scott Act received royal assent, March 30, 1965, the existing Small Tree Act, which protected immature stands, was scrapped, to be replaced by the Forest Improvement Act. The Forest Improvement Act was acknowledged to be an enlightened piece of forest practice legislation, but it was not proclaimed until December 8, 1976, more than a decade later. And for the most part, it has never been enforced.

Prest has come to the conclusion that the Act's unfortunate political fate was no accident: "The Act was brought in as window dressing and to get clear of the Small Tree Act," he charges. "The pulp and paper industry wanted to get rid of the Small Tree Act, and the only way that they could do that was for government to bring in something that appeared better — people wanted protection for their forest."

As a native Nova Scotian, Prest has been appalled at successive governments' lack of will to enforce the Act and to protect the heritage of a naturally productive forest. He says that he feels like the Arab in his childhood school text, who was pushed out of his tent by the camel that wanted to get in out of the sand storm: "In business, it's fine to trust, but it's also wise to be a little practical. Let's put down the rules of the game first. You're welcome into my house, but these are the rules of common courtesy. And when you violate them — out you go. This was never done."

And there are still no house rules. With the scrapping of the Small Tree Act and the propping up in its place of what proved to be a straw man (the Forest Improvement Act), the stage was set for what Prest has characterized as "a full-scale blitzkrieg — 20 years of the most destructive methods of forest harvesting in Nova Scotia's history."

The granting of the tax moratorium, in the absence of protective legislation , proved an invitation to abuse. "I guess any of us would do it," Prest says magnanimously, "if we had a large investment and a five-year tax- free holiday. We would turn as much into money as fast as we could — and that's what happened. They plundered in the worst manner possible, as fast as they could."

Prest, the business man, pretends to understand the exploitation of immature stands. However, he refused to be party to such a policy, even when it was clearly to his financial advantage to do so. On September 16, 1966 (less than a year after the Scott Act was declared), Prest was called to Scott headquarters in Abercrombie for a meeting with Woodlands Manager Bob Murray. Murray spelled out the company's change in policy. For Prest, it amounted to an ultimatum.

"They said we could start at Mooseland and work back as long as we clear-cut everything, or we could go into Lake Charlotte and work out as long as we cut everything. But if we left a tree four inches on the butt and eight feet long, a quarter of a mile over the hill, we had to go get it — she's all coming off.

"Well, that was a shocker, because I couldn't believe after 25 or 30 years of trying to save the country and promote it, that that was going to happen.

"I said that I wasn't buying that deal. In fact, I said, 'Look, if Christ himself came through that door and told me I had to do this, I wouldn't.'"

Prest came home and wrote down the conversation as a way of coping with his own disbelief and to have a record of his version of events for posterity. However, he had to face the reality of the new status quo: If the forest was going to be managed for pulpwood, then there was no future for the sawlog industry. It was just a matter of time. Prest reverted to cutting more on his own land but would not touch his immature stands. He also felt a responsibility to the half-dozen young people who expected to find steady work at his mill, build homes and stake their future in Mooseland: "There's no way I could let them invest, when I could see the end of the line." In 1974, Prest made the hard decision to close the mill. The young people left, and Prest went into retirement.

Prest did not drop from sight, however. He has maintained a high profile in the forestry industry, primarily as a member of the Forest Practices Improvement Board, an advisory body to the Minister of Lands and Forests. He spent his 10-year term, which ended in May 1983, vainly promoting the Forest Improvement Act. Though he no longer has voting privileges, he continues to argue his minority view of forest management in his official role as Acting Consultant to the board.

Prest presents a paradox: He *is* the establishment, and at the same time, he bucks it. A hard-nosed free enterpriser, he espouses the principles of ecological forest management that you expect to hear coming from a less pragmatic environmentalist. He admits to being a stockholder in a multinational company while accusing them of modern-day feudalism. He has been one of the most outspoken critics of the deal struck by the Stanfield Conservatives, and he heaps scorn on the present provincial Conservative administration, describing it as "the most unproductive era in the Department of Lands and Forests history," yet, he unabashedly labels himself as "a lifetime Conservative."

Faced with this snakepit of contradictions, you have to keep in mind that, to Murray Prest, business sense and concern for the future forest are one and the same thing. And most important, his ultimate loyalty is not to any political party, movement or interest group, but to the forest itself. It has been good to him, now he wants to give it something in return.

"We owe the forest something. Somebody my age who has experience, who has studied the thing a lifetime, is duty bound to try to preserve it."

Prest says that his education in forestry began when he set his first rabbit snare and when he caught his first trout. "You might say I have an unfettered view," he quips. "If I'd gone to college, I wouldn't have been a free thinker. I'd have been moulded to that discipline, and it's a discipline that you damn well don't step over."

The discipline that Prest is so bold to challenge is intensive forest management: the classic Canadian pattern of clear-cutting, followed, theoretically at least, by artificial reforestation. To Prest, it spells folly, for it ignores the potential of the natural Acadian forest that is Nova Scotia's rich heritage.

Prest has travelled from the Yukon to the Andes, from California to Europe, and his travels have only served to convince him that Nova Scotia's long-lived species — red spruce, white pine, yellow birch and rock maple — are as good as any trees grown anywhere.

The most lasting impression was made close to home, however. Prest considers himself privileged to have seen the last vestiges of the original Acadian Forest. In the 1950's, there were still 300-year-old stands that had escaped the axes of the original settlers and their successors in the isolated granite country around Mooseland. Because these stands had reached their natural life span and would have been lost to old age if not harvested, Prest cut them. But he never forgot the object lesson they held concerning Nova Scotia's natural forestry potential. "I've seen what can be done. I've seen the virgin hills of yellow birch, and I saw the last of our virgin spruce," Prest says with a zeal that makes you think it was only yesterday that he saw them and not 30 years ago. "Even these old stands that had taken years of beating from the weather and wind were magnificent."

The climax species of the Acadian Forest inspired early settlers to write of "vast cathedrals" and "shady groves of giants." Understandably, most contemporary Nova Scotians cannot think of these rapturous descriptions as anything but romantic hyperbole, or perhaps even fantasy. What they are usually confronted with is the legacy of generations of man's depredation of the forest. It has produced dwarf stands of balsam fir, white spruce and larch — what foresters contemptuously refer to as "sylvan junk."

Nova Scotia has the longest period of logging history in North America. Prest is able to read that history in the forest itself: to him, each stand of trees is a chapter in man's 400-year-long, unfolding story of interaction with the forest.

"I want to show you what they can do to the country," he says as we get into the car for the 15-mile drive to the coast.

Near Tangier on the Eastern Shore, a municipal dump sign marks the site of an old gold-mine works. The hill above it was repeatedly clear cut to feed the mine's steam boilers. Now, it is a mass of spindly balsam fir, 50,000 to 60,000 stems to the acre, few of which will ever reach harvestable size. Prest points out that this is the inevitable result of clear-cutting and, he predicts, a harbinger of tomorrow's forest, if current harvest practices are allowed to continue.

We also follow woods roads to present-day clear-cuts. A number come to a dead end at red spruce stands that, more than anything now, resemble a war scene. Only the stumps, debris of clear-cutting and scrubs remain: "If this is your scientific management," Prest says, surveying the devastation, "it leaves quite a little bit to be desired."

What bothers Prest most is that the regeneration potential of the natural forest is being destroyed. His outrage applies particularly to the red spruce, which has always been the mainstay of the sawlog industry. He staunchly maintains that the species is also the hope for the future of both the pulp (it produces long fibre) and sawmill sectors: "If you manage a forest for sawlogs, everyone else's requirements are met in the process," is his dictum.

Red spruce can grow to a height of 100 feet and remain vigorous for 250 years. Prest has been amazed at the tree's ability to resist disease, animal browsing and insect attack, withstand windstorms and adapt to site conditions. In the granite country, it grows literally on top of boulders, transforming into a sylvan scene an area that otherwise would look like the moonscape of Peggy's Cove. "We used to have a saying that red spruce isn't there because it's good soil, it's good soil because red spruce is there."

For all its virtues, red spruce is more vulnerable than most species to careless harvest techniques, for the simple reason that it reaches harvestable size — at least for pulpwood purposes — before it produces a seed crop. As a result, it is often harvested before it establishes a new generation on the ground. This was graphically illustrated, in one instance, where Scott land abutted Prest's holdings.

On one hand, there was a clear-cut: stumps, bleached grey tops and branches, a few raspberry canes trying to heal the wounds in the earth. But there were no young spruce on the denuded forest floor.

The property line was clearly delineated. Prest's land began where the straight stems of red spruce reached a height of 60 feet. Under the forest canopy, it was cool. The shade had eliminated any competing hardwood vegetation. There was only the all-important moist seedbed of moss, where young spruce seedlings had established a crop for future generations.

Prest selectively cut this stand in 1969. Since then, it has more that doubled its volume, and it will continue to do so every decade, until the trees are at least 150 years old. "It's accumulating interest," the always practical Prest observes.

Prest has no doubt that red spruce stands, managed to ensure natural regeneration, hold out a long-term solution for possible wood shortages in Nova Scotia's future. In essence, that is what he told the provincially convened three-man Royal Commission on Forestry, now in its second year of deliberations on the best course for Nova Scotia's forestry future: "It becomes apparent that the best way to increase the annual growth of merchantable wood is to maintain a crop of trees 10 inches and larger (on the butt), 60 years and older, by selective cutting and not by denuding the land through indiscriminate clear-cutting."

The multinational pulp companies certainly have no intention of switching to a 100-150 rotation. Neither do they need a high-quality tree. They simply want a fast-growing tree for one purpose only — fibre, and cheap fibre at that.

They argue that the best way to meet their industry's goal is through intensive forest management: clear-cutting and artificial reforestation, with the use of herbicides to suppress unwanted competition. The Department of Lands and Forests' reluctance to enforce its own Act seems to provide at least tacit support for this approach, and implementation of the Forest Improvement Act seems more remote all the time. In its brief to the Royal Commission, the department calls the Act "a conundrum" and suggests "review and updating in conjunction with other forestry legislation."

As elsewhere in Canada, the rate of reforestation is falling seriously behind the rate of cutting, and the Lands and Forests' brief confirms that about one-third of the 70,000 acres of forest harvested annually in Nova Scotia does not regenerate naturally. To deal with the problem — which Prest maintains is avoidable in the first place, given disciplined forest practices — the province and the pulp industry have built new tree nurseries and expanded existing facilities. By the mid-1980's, they say, they will be producing 18 to 30 million seedlings annually, enough to reforest the 24,700 acres being laid bare by clear-cutting each year.

If, in fact, the province opts for the artificial reforestation route — which it seems poised to do — then Prest foresees tragic consequences for Nova Scotia's traditional relationship to the forest and for the creatures in the forest.

Prest also envisages forest farms encircled by wire fences. Inside the compound, chemicals have been applied to eliminate any animals that might browse the expensive and supposedly genetically superior seedlings. Outside, a guard has been posted to patrol the perimeter. For the first time in their 400-year history, Nova Scotians will not be free to travel their woods without fear of reprisals. What has been considered an inalienable right will have been lost. Prest has coined a term for this nightmarish scenario: *the interlocking process*. It proceeds by a frighteningly logical series of steps that, once set in motion, can only have one conclusion.

The process begins with clear-cutting. Skidders remove the protective duff or moss layer, creating conditions for the establishment of cover species, such as raspberry and pin cherry. Herbicides are applied to suppress this unwanted competition for softwood — sometimes at the cost of killing valuable yellow birch or rock maple. Dead brush is bulldozed into piles and burned, eliminating niches for wildlife.

The next step is to reforest this man-made barrens artificially. Prest has worked out the costs per acre: site preparation $110, nursery seedlings $108, planting $120. Fertilizer may now have to be added as the natural source of nutrients has been removed by herbicides, bulldozing and fire. Add another $100. To this stage, the total cost is $438 per acre, and says Prest, you are a minimum of 40 years from harvesting your first trees.

Even without calculating the interest on this capital investment over the 40-year growth period — which brings the cost to a staggering $2,900 per standing cord — Prest scoffs at the claim that the artificial forest can meet the pulp and paper industry's stated goal of "cheap fibre forever."

"If this kind of artificial reforestation were profitable in Nova Scotia, or even if it could be expected to produce wood fibre at a reasonable cost," he told the Commission, "industry would carry out a programme of its own. It would not wait for government.

"Clearly, industry does not have enough faith in an artificial forestry programme to consider it an acceptable investment."

With government investment, the link of financial bondage is clasped shut. "If you're going to spend $500 an acre to plant, you're going to guard it jealously," reasons Prest. You cannot afford to have animals browsing expensive seedlings or people inadvertently driving over plantations in snowmobiles.

The inevitable last step is the passage of legislation banning people and animals from the forest (the precedent exists in Scotland). The interlocking process is then complete: clear cut — herbicide — fire — pesticides — financial bondage — and restrictive legislation.

For a few cords of wood, the people of Nova Scotia will have lost a priceless part of their heritage — a consequence that is anathema to Prest, who has always viewed the forest as more than a place to procure logs.

There is a way out of this Kafkaesque bureaucratic cycle — if the fateful first step is not taken. Prest says that forest management must begin with disciplined harvest techniques that complement the natural regeneration of high-value species like red spruce and yellow birch. Otherwise, you are locked into a prohibitively expensive reforestation programme. And people are locked out — in effect, disinherited.

Prest allows that artificial reforestation is justified where the natural potential of the forest to regenerate has been destroyed as in the case of fire barrens, but only then.

"I've always been amazed at the natural ability of the forest to regenerate and to adapt to different site conditions," Prest reflected, as we stood in one of his magnificent red spruce stands.

"If I ever had any doubt about my theories, all I had to do was go to the woods."

THE ENEMY ABOVE

Dark New Brunswick. I first heard that phrase years ago. It takes its meaning from the trees, the dark and brooding softwoods that are the province's economic mainstay. Many of those trees are now blackened and browned; for three decades they have been the fine fodder of the spruce budworm. In the past year I have made many excursions from my Nova Scotia home into neighbouring New Brunswick in an attempt to understand how this unnaturally persistent epidemic is affecting life there. As I drove across the vast flat expanse of the Tantramar Marsh, the land bridge between the two provinces, I imagined crossing over into another troubled country. The deeper I travelled into the realm of political intrigue and personal tragedy — as much the budworm's domain as the fir and spruce woods — the more the phrase Dark New Brunswick came to symbolize the very mood and fate of the New Brunswickers themselves.

There was hardly a person I encountered who had not been affected by the budworm infestation and the 30 years' war of chemical spraying that has tried to keep the insect down. It seems that the budworm outbreak, perversely perpetuated rather than eradicated by the spray, has fuelled a similar outbreak of social disease in the human population. Since Confederation — maybe earlier — Maritimers have cultivated a cynical hardiness in the face of the powers-to-be, a sceptical attitude toward political and corporate ends that I'm well acquainted with in my own community, just 30 miles away from the New Brunswick border. But I found that despair, anxiety, mistrust and fear cut a wide swath through the New Brunswick psyche. And it was not only individuals who had been brushed by the wings of the spray, but whole communities that exhibited a deep-seated set of troubled emotions.

Among the first people I went to see were Jimmy Singleton's parents, James and Joan Singleton, at their farmhouse near the northern milltown of Newcastle, at the mouth of the Miramichi River. It was one of those perfectly clear Indian summer days that seem overburdened with nostalgia — in this case not just remembrance of past times but of loss still suffered.

Jimmy Singleton died on the day after his tenth birthday, June 29, 1979. As of this writing [1982], he was the the most recent child to die of Reye's syndrome in New Brunswick — the last one diagnosed and reported, that is. Earlier I had met with Dr. Ken Rozee, who heads a team of researchers at Dalhousie University in Nova Scotia. They had verified, with blood samples from actual Reye's patients, that the syndrome is sparked by a viral-enhancing effect which they had previously linked to the petrochemical emulsifiers used in the spray.

For the Singletons, it had all started with a mild flu that gave Jimmy a sore stomach; within 48 hours his symptoms had escalated through nausea, confusion, delirium, convulsions and coma until he died due to massive intracranial pressure. Had he managed to survive he would have been severely brain-damaged. The Singletons remember every detail of his illness, including the last mad rush 140 kilometres to the Moncton Hospital at two in the morning.

Their son's convulsions were so strong that James had to ask for help to hold him; James is a big man, over six feet tall and heavily muscled from his labouring job at the Boise Cascade mill in Newcastle. Early diagnosis is crucial to the successful treatment of Reye's syndrome, which progresses so rapidly that drastic action, including cutting open two flaps of the skull to relieve the swelling of the brain, has to be taken. The Singletons remember every suspected cause: it might have been an allergic reaction to the prescription their doctor had already given Jimmy for his stomach. Had Joan forgotten to tell the doctors some crucial part of her son's medical history? Near the end, one of the Moncton doctors asked something that took the Singletons completely by surprise: "Did they spray in your area?"

"I just looked at him and he looked at me," Joan remembers. "I didn't know what they were talking about." She and her husband didn't find out until three weeks after Jimmy's funeral, when they read the cause of his death on the front page of *The Moncton Times.* It is hard to believe, considering the amount of ink and indignation that has flowed over the spray program in the past six years, but that was the first time James and Joan Singleton had heard of Reye's syndrome. Northern New Brunswick, the absolute heart of the province's forest and pulp and paper industries, is even "darker" than the rest.

Government and Provincial pulp and paper companies have been spraying to control budworm in the New Brunswick forests since 1952. The only thing that has changed from year to year is the insecticide. From 1952 until 1968 DDT was the chemical used; when its long-term deleterious effects on the environment became clear in the mid-1960s, an organophosphate compound called phosphamidon was phased in. It was the predominate spray for the next decade, then it too was replaced by a supposedly safer organophosphate spray called fenitrothion. Fenitrothion is now the chemical of choice, although Matacil (a carbamate) was used on a wide scale in 1979 when fenitrothion temporarily fell from favour while the New Brunswick government ordered health tests on it. Like it or not, New Brunswickers are caught up in a fickle game of chemical chairs.

The names blur and are hard to pronounce, but one thing to remember is that both types of sprays used since 1968 (the organophosphates and the carbamates) are neurotoxins. They block the enzyme cholinesterase, which is essential to the transmission of nerve impulses in all organisms, from insects to man. They work on the budworm by knocking the larvae off the trees — once on the ground they are unable to get back to the buds and new growth, so they starve. The sprays also "knock down" bees, wasps, spiders and birds and other natural predators of the budworm. Research on human beings exposed to chronic low levels of these kinds of insecticides shows that they suffer a higher than normal level of nervous disorders and a greater incidence of leucopenia (low white blood cell count) which makes them more susceptible to infectious diseases. No general health study of the province has ever been done, but the very least that can be said is that New Brunswickers are a population at risk.

In 1981 alone, 1.5 million pounds of fenitrothion (not counting the other chemical components of the spray, the solvents and emulsifiers) were sprayed over 7,000 square miles of the province. A one-mile setback zone (since modified to 1,000 feet) from human habitation was established in 1977 but it hardly provides adequate protection when a "good" spray is considered one in which half of the chemical arrives on target. The other half drifts in the wind and has been found in rainwater 50 miles from the nearest spray block. The best available data indicated that as little as three percent and sometimes more than double the dose can land within the target area.

Before 1976, the debate on the efficiency of the budworm spray program and its possible environmental and health effects was basically an insiders' argument between two camps promoting competing interpretations of "good" forest management. The corporate model, which was sponsored and spawned by big business, government and the Canadian Forestry Service, believed that the forest was a farm and should be treated as such. Level it in the cheapest and quickest way possible (clearcut with big machines), plant it (using herbicides to keep out the weed varieties and pesticides to keep insects away), let it grow for its 40 years to maturity and then go in and harvest. Start again.

The other model, known as silviculture, called for selective cutting of mature trees and planting to get the forest back into a healthy semblance of its pre-20th century self. It was labour intensive — prone to the chainsaw rather than the chemical approach to "control". In other words, to silviculturists the forest had to be treated like a forest.

Even the corporate woodsmen agreed that the object of spraying wasn't to get rid of the spruce budworm. There didn't seem to be a way to wipe the insect out, since spraying seemed to keep the insect at permanent semi-epidemic levels by preserving the mature trees for its food supply. The budworm would never starve. But with the attitude that the trees were a crop that the forestry industry had a right to harvest, the crop had to be protected; thus year after year of stopgap spraying, and ever increasing areas of budworm infestation.

Until 1976, the New Brunswick people were fairly acquiescent about spraying. The industry and government could take care of the industry because, after all, the industry took care of New Brunswickers. In 1982 there were 15,000 jobs directly involved, and another 20,000 indirectly. The forest industry contributed almost $1 billion a year to the provincial economy in a normal year. It represented more than two thirds of the province's exports in foreign markets, affecting its balance of payments. In short, it is a very critical foundation resource to the wellbeing of all New Brunswickers.

But in 1976 several events conspired to give birth to the first antispray protest group in New Brunswick and the first citizens' assault on the status quo. The first studies of the Dalhousie research team, establishing what was then only a probable link between Reye's syndrome and the spray, became public knowledge in the spring of '76, sparking the first intensive public scrutiny of the budworm war. Nova Scotia had never sprayed and had weathered two previous epidemics in the century, but was under extreme pressure from the forest industry to spray to control an epidemic then raging in the Cape Breton highlands. With the added impetus of the revealed health hazards, a citizens' protest group in Cape Breton successfully countered every argument that the forest industry brought to bear, even the threat by Nova Scotia Forest Industries (NSFI), owned by the Swedish multinational Stora Kopparberg, that it would have to move right out of Nova Scotia in five years if spraying of its wood supply wasn't undertaken immediately. Since there was no legacy of spraying to counter, the Cape Bretoners could argue about economics first and possible health hazards later, so they were effective at meeting both industry and Gerald Regan's Liberal provincial government on businesslike ground. As the group's economic and supply forecasts predicted, six years later NSFI is still able to operate in Cape Breton and the budworm epidemic has collapsed on its own.

In New Brunswick the issue was much more visceral. At the same time as the Dalhousie research was making headlines, Forest Protection Limited (FPL), the government-and-industry-run company that handles the annual spray campaign, was gearing up for the largest spray ever — 9.5 million acres of New Brunswick forests. You didn't have to be in the fields or woods that spring to be at risk; planes seemed to spray with impunity, fighting the good fight over fields, lakes, houses and even schoolyards. One schoolyard was sprayed during recess in the small town of Hampton, near Saint John in southern New Brunswick, and over the next seven months three of the children developed meningo-encephalitis. Two of the three subsequently died, with symptoms similar to those of Reye's syndrome. Simply and appropriately, the anti-spray group born in response to this incident was called Concerned Parents.

Concerned Parents represented the beginnings of public opposition to the official sanction of the spray and they paid a personal price of character attacks for their views. "We have been quite hysterically accused of being irrational," quips Catherine Richards, researcher of the group since its inception and perhaps more responsible than any of its 300 or so active members for its public credibility. "We're always accused of being emotional. I think it's because we called ourselves *parents* and a lot of us are women so that the label was an easy one to apply."

Richards, a housewife and mother in her mid-30's, is without question the most knowledgeable lay person on the budworm issue in New Brunswick, a kind of Stanley Knowles of the budworm world. The dining room of her suburban Fredericton house is her research centre. An office filing cabinet holds court, stuffed to overflowing with reprints of scientific papers touching on almost any aspect of the budworm question — in her cheerful and fastidious way she can lay her hands on any one you might want at a moment's notice.

Take this one for instance: In the spring of 1980 Richards got her hands on a hard-to-come-by translation of a Japanese study (conducted by Dr. Takashi Kawachi of the National Research Centre of Cancer in Japan) which showed that fenitrothion caused both mutations and chromosome aberrations. Of 25 chemicals ranked according to their strength in mutation and chromosome aberration tests, fenitrothion ranked second and sixth respectively. It produced significant chromosome breakage in rat bone marrow when administered to live rats, and also affected chromosomes in human embryo cells. Concerned Parents thought these results particularly disturbing because the Sumitomo Chemical Company, a manufacturer of fenitrothion, has claimed that it is "completely devoid" of mutagenic activity. Richards also pointed out that fenitrothion is one of the 100 suspect chemicals on the Industrial Biotest (IBT) list. In 1977 the U.S. company was found to have falsified tests, and as a result all of its testing (which the Canadian government depended on in its decisions to license chemicals) is currently under review in the U.S. and Canada. Two-thirds of the IBT studies reviewed so far have been found invalid.

This information disseminated by Concerned Parents takes on significance in light of cancer rates for New Brunswick released by Statistics Canada in 1981 (based on 1977 data). Richards publicized the figures, which show that New Brunswick's overall rate of new cases of cancer is greater than the Canadian average. And even though for all intents and purposes the two Maritime provinces share the same climate, landscape and genetic stock, New Brunswick's rate was one-third higher than Nova Scotia's. Health Minister Brenda Robertson's reaction to the cancer rate was to say that one can't be too simplistic when evaluating such statistics — perhaps the higher New Brunswick rates were due to better detection on the part of the province's doctors. When it was pointed out to her that a doctor in New Brunswick serves 922 patients on average while Nova Scotia doctors handle only 560, Robertson stood her ground: "It's very easy to say that they're spread more thinly, but I can't agree that their diagnosis is going to be less accurate. I would suggest that our doctors work a lot longer hours than if we had more doctors."

"It's kind of funny," Richards says. "It's the way politicians work — you say something and they twist it just a little bit and they answer what they twisted rather than what you really said."

Even so, Concerned Parents has had its victories: The acreage sprayed in 1977 was reduced by half from the record previous year, and the group can accept credit for that government concession. The now-wavering setback zone was also established in 1977, and because of Concerned Parents' loud protests the spraying concerns try as best as they can to avoid flying their loads of pesticide mist over private land in southern New Brunswick. But the group has been nowhere near as successful as its counterpart in Nova Scotia, and this is directly attributable to the fact that the pro-spraying forces in New Brunswick are an institutionalized part of the province's life. The departments of Natural Resources, Environment and Health, the Canadian Forestry Service's Maritime branch based in Fredericton, Forest Protection Limited and the pulp and paper companies, the Hatfield Conservative government which has held office 11 years — all are wrapped up in the warp and weft of a pro-spray forestry policy.

Perhaps a look at FPL is the best way to explain how it all works. Formed in 1952 by the government in cooperation with the industry, FPL's board is still dominated by ministers of the Crown and executives of the pulp companies, including Bud Bird, Brenda Robertson and Gordon Baskerville, the new Assistant Deputy Minister of Natural Resources. H.J. (Bud) Irving, the former forest

100

firefighter and pilot who is now managing director of FPL, sets out the flow chart: "Although it has a share structure, the shares are owned over 90 percent by the government through the Department of Natural Resources and less than 10 per cent by the forest industry. We operate as a non-profit organization....

"Approximately two-thirds of the funding comes from the province and one-third from the nine pulp and paper companies. The government at all times appoints the majority of the board of directors. So for all practical purposes we are controlled by the provincial government." The actual areas to be sprayed, Irving says, are figured out by the Department of Natural Resources, in consultation with the Canadian Forestry Service (which does the egg-mass counts on the budworm) and industry. The status quo is very interdependent, and in essence controlled by the elected representatives of the people.

Concerned Parents has tried the litigation route against FPL and discovered through a protracted and expensive court action that the laws of the land seem constituted to provide better protection to animals and fishes than to people. In March 1977, they laid 31 separate charges against FPL arising from the 1976 spray season, under both the Federal Fisheries Act and the Pest Control Products Act (PCP). FPL responded by arguing before the Supreme Court of New Brunswick that it was an agent of the Crown and thus immune from such charges.

The Supreme Court ruled that FPL was not an agent of the Crown and turned the case back to the local magistrates for the trial. FPL appealed and won half its point — the Appeal Court ruled in May 1979 that the Fisheries Act does bind FPL but that the Pest Control Products does not. Both FPL and Concerned Parents sought leave to appeal that decision to the Supreme Court of Canada, but leave was denied both of them.

FPL has one more manoeuvre up its sleeve. It sought a stay of proceedings with respect to the charges it still faced under the Fisheries Act. The stay was granted in May 1980 and remains in effect. Concerned Parents might have pressed ahead against that last decision, but decided it wasn't worth the effort or the money. Instead they are lobbying hard for an amendment that has been given first reading in the House of Commons that would make the PCP Act binding on the Crown.

It is naive of Concerned Parents to be indignant about this three-year, wear-you-down legal battle — that's how these kinds of things are fought. But Clark Phillips, a wood lot owner and organic farmer who chaired Concerned Parents' legal committee, is bitter about the outcome and worried about the consequences: "This is supposed to be a society of law, with democratic input into the structure of law. When one piece of society, this consortium of pulp companies held together with the government glue called FPL, develops for itself a position of absolute power, it can prompt a kind of desperate individual action."

Reasonable individual action is certainly hard to take, and confined to the few New Brunswickers who can afford it. In 1976, Abram Friesen, a University of New Brunswick professor who lives on a farm 13 kilometres from Fredericton, did win a shortlived moral victory when he successfully sued FPL for trespass, nuisance and negligence. He and his family had been enjoying one of the New Brunswick rites of spring, picking fiddleheads on their property, when another of those rites passed over their heads and soused them with fenitrothion. Abe and his wife, Marie-Luise, developed acute symptoms of pesticide poisoning and the next day their 11-year-old son suffered a severe asthma attack. All three required medical attention. The Friesens were outraged, especially because they had requested and received written assurance from FPL that their property would be exempt from the spray area.

After a year of hearings the Friesens were awarded $1,328 in damages. It had cost them 25 times that much to prove their case — $32,000. Even with the court costs awarded to them they are still out $10,000, a financial burden that the average New Brunswicker could not consider incurring. And what's worse is that their successful day in court had the long-term effect of further diminishing the rights of the individual to challenge FPL's practices.

The New Brunswick government responded to the Friesen precedent by immediately proposing a special bill which would have given FPL powers to spray anywhere in the province — including private property and in spite of owner's wishes. It also advocated removal of the landowner's right to lay claim to damages. The measure proved too Draconian even for the New Brunswick political climate, and the government was forced to introduce an amendment which allowed actions against FPL for trespass — but only when damages to property could be proven. That is something which, Clark Phillips points out, is very hard to do. "We received a New Brunswick kind of justice," says Abe Friesen.

Most New Brunswickers are not in a position to speak out for others. Many do not even have the option of defending themselves. A character in a book by New Brunswick writer Alden Nowlan, himself the son of a pulp cutter, uttered the survivor's creed of the lower-class Maritimer: "You keep you mouth shut and your ass close to the ground." And look what happens when you trespass against that creed, even in southern New Brunswick where public activism has made inroads.

Don Morris has lived all his 27 years in New Brunswick and spring isn't spring to him without spraying. He remembers as a child the planes flying low over the farmyard and his father wiping DDT from the windshield of the car. He inherited his father's 125 acre farm, much of which is woodlot, in Ford Mills, Kent County, an economically depressed area in the southeastern part of the province. Don does as his father did before him, cuts pulp in the winter and keeps a few animals. If he lived elsewhere he might be called a homesteader but here that is definitely an outsider's term.

Don's own woodlot is budworm damaged ("It doesn't matter what size fir I cut, the heart is rotten"), but he is not complacent about the thought of being sprayed: "I've heard of woodsworkers in the Salmon River area getting sprayed but they don't seem to mind, like they're big tough lumbermen or something. They take the government's word — they trust these people." What happened to his 25-year-old wife Pamela last summer as she worked planting trees for the government is proof enough for Don that any trust is misplaced.

Most of the treeplanters in the area are women. Though lugging trays of 300 seedlings while you plant is heavy work, competition for the jobs is keen. Pam, who held the job the summer before, felt pretty lucky to be rehired for 1981 on the basis of her good reputation — even though her crew was told by District Ranger Ed Parkhill that there was a possibility they would be sprayed because the planting area, along the Salmon River Road, was within the spray area. If they were worried, said Parkhill, they could call the

Zenith number of FPL for the daily spraying schedule and stay home for a day without pay.

Pam did stay home on June 3rd to be out of harm's way when the planes went over. On June 4th, she finished her day's work by 11:30 a.m. and was waiting for others in the crew, including her sister Johanne Amyotte, to walk back along the woods road with her to the cars. She looked up at the sound of engines and saw two planes flying low over the treeline toward the open planting areas. One of them still had its spray nozzles open. Planter Debbie Agnew, working right under the flightline, was drenched in the chemical mist. "They should have seen us," admitted duty ranger Dave Clark. "There were four cars along the treeline and my service truck — they should have seen that at least."

Pam Morris was so upset that she headed for the cars in tears, and Clark told her that to reassure herself she should give his boss Ed Parkhill a call. Parkhill was surprised by the accident, and told Pam to see a doctor if she wished. Pam also called a friend for advice, and perhaps wishes now she hadn't. The friend was connected to the anti-spray network, and got in touch immediately with Concerned Parents. The accident was reported on radio that afternoon and Pam Morris unintentionally became the leading figure in the breaking story.

Official reaction was swift. A directive came from the regional office of the Department of Natural Resources requiring that all those on the plantation that morning go for a specific kind of blood test (plasma pseudocholinesterase testing) considered reliable at detecting fenitrothion exposure. Pam and five co-workers went to the Rexton Medical Centre that evening to have samples taken by the public health nurse. The nurse could not get enough of a sample from Debbie Agnew, the one who had been doused, so she went to a doctor in Moncton the next morning where a sample was taken. Pam Morris and her sister, just to be on the safe side — because after all you never can tell — got a second set of blood samples taken at Rexton the next morning. In all, three sets of blood samples were taken — two done in Rexton and one in Moncton, where the Regional Laboratory is located.

Three weeks passed before a letter dated June 25 arrived from Dr. Albert Fraser of the regional lab to say that the samples had been "discarded by mistake prior to analysis. If required, please send another sample." Debbie Agnew remembers, "Pam called me

104

and said hers was lost. The next morning I got a phone call that the sample I had done in Moncton had been misplaced. When I found out all the ones from Rexton were lost too I thought it was kind of funny."

Spokesmen for the Department of Health and Moncton Hospital, which houses the regional lab, thought it kind of funny too, but the only explanation I got from them when researching this story was "An error was made" — until I made it clear to Fred Rayworth, public relations officer for the hospital, that not just one set of samples but three separate batches had been lost. He got in touch with Albert Fraser of the lab, who quickly got in touch with me. Fraser said that all the samples had been batched and placed in the lab freezer (a common practice for infrequently done tests) so that they could be analyzed at the same time when the lab's senior technologist got back from vacation. Fraser didn't know how they came to be discarded, just that when the technologist got back on the job they were nowhere to be found.

The lab processes approximately 100,000 tests a month and understandably a few are lost or broken. But it only processes 40 to 50 cholinesterase tests a year, and this was the first time the lab had lost any. Fraser told me that at least two other samples, from greenhouse workers in Hillsborough, had been tossed out with the Rexton batch: "This proves that there was no conspiracy to deliberately discard the Rexton samples."

For Pamela Morris, who did or didn't do what and when seems purely academic now. Shy and thin, with a redhead's pale complexion, she was obviously depressed the last time I talked with her, speaking in even shyer halting tones. It seems that the Department of Natural Resources had fired her a month after the incident for failing two regular department inspections of her work in the category of "firmness". (Foreman Doris Scott told me: "I'm up and down between the rows all the time. Anytime I inspected her work it was all right. She was a real good planter. I was surprised when she failed, really surprised, especially the second time.") Two strikes and she was out, but a third was sent her way. She had just found out that she was pregnant with her second child, due in February of 1982 — meaning that the baby might have been conceived before she was sprayed.

Things in general are not easy with the Morrises. The loss of Pam's job jeopardizes their financial security — it has been nearly two years since Don held a paying job off the farm. There is little hope of her being rehired as a planter on her "good" reputation this year, and she has resigned herself to it: "That's the situation we're in. A lot of people have put up with being sprayed." The unspoken thought is that if they don't, they suffer more than just the consequences of the spray.

John LaBossiere, a neighbour of Pam and Don Morris, lives a few miles away in Bass River, where he is trying to get a farm going, and substitute teaches in Rexton to make ends meet. In 1980, LaBossiere stepped down after four years as leader of the provincial NDP party, the most thankless job in New Brunswick politics, for at the time, the NDP had yet to secure a single seat. But it gave LaBossiere a podium from which to broadcast his opposition to the spray.

Of the three major New Brunswick political parties, the NDP under LaBossiere was alone in its anti-spray policy. LaBossiere thinks that his former political colleagues don't share his views simply because they are misinformed: "My impression of politicians in New Brunswick is that there are only a few who do their own research and that a great number of them rely on existing sources to tell them about the forest industry." He lists those sources as the chemical manufacturers, and even the five English-language daily papers, some radio stations and the CBC-TV affiliate in Saint John, which are owned by the powerful K.C. Irving empire, whose forestry holdings are the largest in the province. All, he points out, have a considerable vested interest in the spray program.

So LaBossiere can understand the average New Brunswicker's quiet acceptance of the status quo: "What can you expect of people in a poor province whose economic wellbeing is controlled by a small number of people? Obviously you are going to be reluctant to speak out in public because your entire future can be jeopardized by what you say."

Any cruise of the power grid in New Brunswick would be incomplete without a stop to consider the inscrutable and reclusive Irving family. There is K.C. himself, who caused a certain amount of provincial indignation by retiring right out of the province and into a life in the Bahamas in 1971. And there is his trio of middle-aged executive sons, James, Arthur and John, who between them, control vast interests in every sector of the provincial economy. Nobody has yet succeeded in compiling a corporate flow chart; it is simply true that in New Brunswick K.C. Irving's interests matter most.

J.D. Irving Ltd. is the forestry sector, reputedly the largest such company in the world, with holdings covering an estimated million acres of New Brunswick. They are so big that although they are part of the industrial group contributing to FPL they also run their own spray operation, Forest Patrol Limited, easy to confuse with the government operation because it shares the same initials. Forest Patrol Limited sprays each year for budworm — after it finds out what FPL plans to cover — but it hasn't used the viral-enhancing emulsifiers with its fenitrothion for six years. David Oxley, woodlands manager for J.D. Irving Ltd., says, "We feel we are moving in the right direction being able to drop the emulsifier component, which was becoming controversial."

But 10 percent of their spray program involves applying broadleaf herbicide to J.D. Irving's $10-million annual reforestation program — and controversy is where they are headed. In 1980 Forest Patrol Limited sprayed 17,865 acres of New Brunswick with 2,4,5-T when it had a permit from the Department of Environment to treat only 12,357 acres. "We were definitely concerned," says Kenneth Browne, head of Environment's Toxic Substances Branch. "We found out where those acres were and checked to see that they met conditions of setback from habitation and water courses. But, as the company explained, they didn't anticipate that they would need to treat all the acres that they did.

"It was probably a violation," Browne admits. "They acknowledge it but there is no way of taking them to court because we didn't witness it." Brown says the situation has been corrected. In future the company simply will "overestimate" the number of acres it wants to treat. So it's more or less all up to J.D. Irving — which hardly reflects a cautious approach on the part of the government to the use of a chemical that has been banned in a number of European countries (Norway, Sweden, Italy, the Netherlands) and has been severely restricted in the U.S. following an Oregon study which connected miscarriages to its use as a forest spray. In fact, some of the 2,4,5-T in question was purchased by Irving from Ontario Hydro after the chemical had been banned in that province.

The Department of Environment did successfully prosecute Forest Patrol Limited in May 1981 for "flagrantly" disregarding

Section 16 of the provincial Pesticides Act, by spraying Roundup — a new and relatively untested herbicide — without a permit. In fining the company $200 (maximum sentence would have been $1,000 or 100 days in jail), Provincial Court Judge Donald Allen said: "To flagrantly disregard the section of the Pesticides Act would be to use the chemical without knowledge of its effects. They knew what they were doing but it was too late to obtain a permit." It seems that the public interest in these matters is being constantly entrusted to the discretion of J.D. Irving Ltd. And J.D. Irving is certainly aware that it needs to inspire this trust.

The illegal spraying of Roundup took place in Dubee Settlement, southern New Brunswick, a mile from the head of Millstream. It is hard to say where Millstream begins and ends, just that for several miles from the head to a place called Berwick Corner houses are strung like beads along the river. Pastureland slopes up to wooded hills and cows graze: this is the centre of Sussex farmland well known throughout the Maritimes for its dairy products. It is appealingly pastoral, beautiful, calm, but Millstream is both a repository of all the common fears of New Brunswickers about the chemical management of their forests and the source of some of the most outspoken antispray protest.

Paul and Madeline Taylor moved to Millstream in 1975 after Paul, a United Church minister, accepted charge of the circuit of local churches. Their first spring, spray planes flew close to their house. The manse was not plastered with fenitrothion as were some of the neighbouring homes, but inside the manse were the Taylors' five children. "I thought, I can't be a good mother if I don't fight this thing," says Madeline. She soon joined the fledgling Concerned Parents Group. Commitment to her children led to commitment to a cause — last spring she was elected president.

Madeline is a nurse. Her part-time shifts at Sussex Hospital and her involvement in local church work brought her face to face with what she sees as a phenomenon of ill health in her pretty little community. "I have never lived in a place that discussed health so much," she told me. "It seems there's always something to do with sickness or death. You can just go down the road," she said with a sweep of her arm as we sat on the manse verandah looking out on summer fields, and she began to list the illnesses which had touched each neighbouring house: women who suffered a rare blood disease, brain cancer, a mastectomy; a young man with cancer of the testes; a young girl with lung cysts.

Her gesture has extended further. She has searched the local church records and discovered that since 1969, of 41 deaths not attributable to old age, 14 were due to cancer and four were stillbirths. At a United Church Women's meeting one evening she looked around the room and realized that out of 12 women present four had been treated for breast cancer. Another member had died recently of breast cancer and still another of intestinal cancer. She knows that there is not enough comparable information about the health of the general population in New Brunswick or the rest of Canada for her informal surveying to be significant scientifically, but she firmly believes her friends and neighbours have been victims of their environment, saturated with three decades of chemical spraying. As a result, she has dedicated herself to overcoming the persistent air of fatalism within the community of Millstream.

She has had some success. Madeline Taylor's lobbying within her own profession, with help from another Concerned Parents member, physiotherapist Peggy Land, resulted in the Sussex medical community becoming the first in New Brunswick to officially state its opposition to the spray. In February 1981, 69 health care workers, including seven doctors, signed a petition calling on government to discontinue the spray program because " its questionable effectiveness does not justify the risks to human health." That may not seem like much of a radical move, but it has in effect isolated medical workers in Sussex from their provincial colleagues. Despite the fact that in 1976 the Nova Scotia Medical Society decided that there was enough proof of harmful effects on health to come out strongly against aerial spraying, the New Brunswick Medical Society has not yet uttered a peep. When asked if the Rozee human tissue research into Reye's might change medical minds, spokesperson Dr. John Bennett said that the society is waiting for Rozee's study to be validated, presumably by the government-appointed panel headed by McGill pharmacologist Dr. Donald Ecobichon, since the society has no funds for such work: "When it is validated I think people will have something on which to make a decision. But as long as there are pros and cons being put forward it is very difficult to be dogmatic as to what is right or wrong."

Dr. Sol Khederi, one of the Sussex doctors to sign the petition, defends the stand he took: "We felt that until you could prove something is safe you don't use it. They say the chemicals haven't been shown to be harmful — that's basically a negative argument. They haven't been checked to any extent....It surprises me that things like 2,4,5-T that have been banned elsewhere are readily used here. It seems that in New Brunswick, we have become a dumping ground." A rider on the Sussex medical petition called for an immediate ban on the use of herbicides such as 2,4,5-T that contain dioxin.

Herbicides have nothing to do with the budworm spray program and everything to do with large scale industrial forest management. Herbicides have become another issue in this environmental war. Madeline Taylor heard that J.D. Irving Ltd. had applied to spray 150 acres at the head of Millstream with 2,4,5-T in June and she quickly circulated a petition. Widespread community support brought the Sussex Town Council on side — and not only drew a retraction of the Irving plans but brought James, K.C.'s eldest son and head of the forestry sector, out to Millstream on a hot July morning , something unheard of in the annals of reclusive Irvingdom.

I happened to be in luck. I had got to Clark Phillips' the evening before (and stayed up half the night while Clark reviewed the history of Concerned Parents' court battles for me) and was there at 7:30 on July 23 when Madeline called with the news that James Irving was flying in for a meeting.

I got to Berwick Corner in half an hour. It was already hot and I was glad to slip into the cool rooms of the manse, where Madeline was busy tidying up in preparation for her guest. Two other Millstream women arrived: Peggy Land and Ursula Becker, a local farmer. We went out on the verandah where we chatted until we heard the concussive beating of the helicopter blades. Madeline crossed the yard to the abandoned pastures where the helicopter set down. None of us could quite believe that this was happening, and everyone seemed as much amused as intimidated by the spectacle.

Jim Irving came back across the field following Madeline. A tall, heavy-set man dressed casually in short rain jacket, grey flannels, blue shirt and garish paisley tie, the first thing he said after introductions had been made was almost maudlin:"I'm interested in growing trees."

He then proceeded to give us a short course in reforestation. He needed sprays like 2,4,5-T to kill broadleaf growth in stands of young fir and spruce so that the hardwoods would not smother out the seedlings. Herbicides were indispensable to his company's reforestation programs. In fact J.D. Irving has been using broadleaf herbicides (2,4-D and 2,4,5-T formulations) since the late 1950s. In 1981, 34,000 acres were treated. Irving ended his lecture rhetorically: "You really believe that these chemicals are dangerous?"

Peggy Land replied that dioxin, a contaminant in 2,4,5-T, was considered by some scientists as the most deadly chemical known to man. Irving deferred graciously:"I see that you know more about this than we do. If we've done something wrong we want to change it." However, Irving had not come to concede that his company practices were hazardous, nor to offer his apologies for any wrong doing. He had a proposition to make: His company would fund a study of the health hazards of 2,4,5-T. He appealed to the women to keep an open mind, and asked that if his study demonstrated that the herbicide was safe, they would publicly acknowledge their mistake.

After the helicopter lifted off, I stood in the manse yard with Ursula Becker. She was sceptical: "I think that Irving already knows that there is something wrong, that there may come a time that people say 'We are hurt.' He needs something to protect him. He wants to have it in black and white that he did everything right. It cost a lot of money. It must be worth something to him." The next day I read in papers owned by Irving that Concerned Parents had agreed to cooperate with the company on a safety study of herbicides.

The next time I saw Ursula was in November. I drove with her and Madeline Taylor to the source of the Shack Brook, which spills from the high wooded ground behind the Becker farm into their pasture and is the sole source of water for their 125-head Holstein herd. Below the Becker property it runs into Millstream. The brook was the Beckers' private symbol for the pristine character of their adopted country when they moved to New Brunswick from West Germany in November 1975. Lothar Becker chose the location of

111

the farm because there was no one living up stream of the spring-fed water source:" I thought, it's nice, no one's peeing in my brook."

Ursula steered the half ton truck through the tight turns of the rainsoaked and deeply rutted woods road. Several miles in back of the Becker farm we came upon a clearcut area — Irving ground. A hundred acres, give or take a few, had been levelled. Since it was November, I had expected to see the broadleaf vegetation wilted, but the women explained that the young saplings were black even in mid-summer. The only green was of new-growth softwoods emerging from the tangle of rotted vegetation and uprooted dead-wood.

Ursula took a branch road to the right and parked the truck on a ridge. Below us was the Shack Brook, bisecting the herbicide treated plantation. A stone's throw from where it crossed the road was its source among the only mature trees left standing in this virtual wasteland. The land sloped toward the brook from both sides and it was obvious that any run-off would find its way into the brook. "I believe that the problems we saw this year are due to the fact that J.D. Irving sprayed Roundup there," Ursula said. "They sprayed here since 1952 with fenitrothion but for herbicide spray it was the first year, last year."

Since May 1981 the Becker herd has produced seven sets of twins and 11 of these calves have been stillborn. "It makes me bankrupt, you know," Lothar told me. "If you have seven sets of twins in one year that would be all right. But if they come back-wards and they're stuck — we're just lucky that we get the cows through all right." Besides the high rate of twinning and stillbirths, the Holsteins have also had infertility and abortion problems of late. Two cows aborted in midterm in July 1981; in September a hairless calf was born prematurely at six months. Many cows have not been conceiving when bred either by artificial insemination or by bull. Lothar has no explanation — the feeding and breeding regimens are the same as in previous years. Neither does veterinarian Dr. Ian Leask, who says that tests have turned up no infectious cause for the abortions. "For now," he says, "I put the twinning down to stats. I'm not saying that these herbicides couldn't be causing it, but I would be going out on a limb if I said they were."

A long limb indeed, because no one is sure of the possible health effects of Roundup. In fact Agriculture Canada, which licenses all experimental permits for chemicals like these, stopped okaying experimental permits for Roundup in 1981. They hand out permits for two reasons: first to test the efficacy of the chemical — does it work? — and, second, to test health and safety. Enough permits had been granted to prove Roundup effective at killing broadleaf vegetation, but none had been granted to test for effects on health so Agriculture Canada said to pause a while. In 1980, under experimental permits, nearly 10,000 acres were sprayed with Roundup in New Brunswick and the permits allowed spraying within 250 feet of habitation. The Monsanto Chemical Company claims that Roundup (glyphosate) is "relatively non-persistent." But the U.S. Environmental Protection Agency (EPA) has asked that all studies on Roundup be repeated. Monsanto in turn has sued the EPA to prevent release of registration data on the chemical to the public. Its toxicity is definitely in question, and it is one of the names on the suspected chemical list of Industrial Biotest.

The Beckers' health problems have not only been with their cattle. Here is a list of recent family ailments: Since July 1980, their son Martin has been hospitalized three times. He has suffered convulsions and lost consciousness briefly during the last episode. No diagnosis has been made though food poisoning has been suggested. "They don't know what it is," Ursula says. " He runs a high fever and vomits. It seems to me that he is sensitive to something and we don't know what it is." Ursula herself has undergone exploratory surgery for a gall-bladder ailment of unknown etiology. In all, members of the family have been hospitalized six times within a year. Before coming to Canada they were healthy.

The events of last year prompted Ursula, already active in Concerned Parents, to go out into her community to conduct a health survey. She has interviewed all of her neighbours within a three-mile radius. At first people were reluctant to cooperate: "People have shame about sickness. They want to appear healthy and happy." says Ursula. But the ideal community image was far more real. She tabulated a distressing number of complaints — 70 described by sufferers as serious out of a population of 170. Lung problems, including asthma, emphysema and persistent colds, predominated. Ursula's scribbler delivered another count: five birth defects, one stillbirth, four miscarriages and three premature births.

What Ursula Becker and Madeline Taylor perceive as a phenomenon of illness in their community is unsubstantiated. But the insidious fear shared by many in Millstream that three decades of spraying is now taking its toll is tragic in itself. People in Millstream think that they have a right to know whether their health is being endangered by government policy. And they also know that not knowing what is undermining their health — Is it in their heads? Is it really happening? Is it the same anywhere else? — can sometimes be worse than being faced with a definite diagnosis.

Newcastle, Bathurst, Campbellton and Dalhousie: all northern New Brunswick milltowns, and very little in between except the forests that feed the mills. As I drove north from Newcastle where I had visited Jimmy Singleton's parents, the arguments concerning the economic imperatives of spraying became more nagging. I wondered whether the proponents of the spray might at least be partially justified in saying that "southerners can afford their doom-saying."

The settlements interspersed between the milltowns are poor; their reason for being is not readily apparent. Occasionally I saw a log skidder parked in a back yard, but realized that the owner probably contracted for multinational pulp companies. The small mills are dying: four of the six in the Miramichi River area have closed. Unemployment is almost palpable as you pass through the villages of this economic outback. Dalhousie is as far north as you can get in New Brunswick. There's no question that it is a milltown. The New Brunswick International Paper Company (NBIP) — formerly Canadian International Paper, the instigator of the spray program back in 1952 — takes up one whole side of the main street. There is a mountain of pulp constantly in the making as a river of barked logs spills from a mammoth conveyor. In the background are the silhouettes of the Quebec mountains that hem in the Baie des Chaleurs.

Len Clifford grew up in Dalhousie and like many native sons went to work in the NBIP mill after high school. In the early '70s he headed out west to work for a few years, but he and his wife Marsha (also Dalhousie-born) always wanted to return to New Brunswick to raise their family — Natasha, 9, Crystal Dawn, 7, and Lenwood, 2. In 1976, they came home to build a bungalow on a farm in St. Maure, a little community 15 miles inland from Dalhousie. And in 1980, after four years of knocking on the door, Len got his old job back at the mill. Things seemed to be working out for the Cliffords, until this spring when a close encounter with the spray shook their confidence in their future in New Brunswick.

The incident is like most of the others. Len had requested that his property be exempt from the spray and had received a letter of confirmation when he was awakened by the sound of planes flying near his house. He headed off to the local airport and after some trouble found out that the nearest spray zone to his house was two miles away. But when he got home that night: "The planes were spraying right in my back yard. So we took off and went to a hotel for the evening. The next day we came back and the children got sick."

So they took off again, this time to the Quebec side of the Baie des Chaleurs for a few days but when they came back home the baby, Lenwood, got sick and this time had to be hospitalized. "The doctor couldn't say for sure it wasn't the spray, but he couldn't say it was. It was just sort of mysterious to him," says Marsha. "But it was an awful coincidence for it to recur when we got home. Would the flu do that?"

The Cliffords decided that maybe they should get their well water checked for fenitrothion, and the Department of Health sent an inspector from Campbellton, but he came equipped to test for bacteria only. "He told us the water was potable," Len said with a chuckle. Then their inquiries got bounced from the Department of the Environment to Natural Resources and back, and it was only when Len applied to MLA Allen Maher for help (and Maher raised the incident in the legislature) that Environment began to monitor the water in the Clifford's well. Five tests have all indicated traces of fenitrothion in the family's tap water, and the latest, performed in January this year, registered the highest reading — .9 parts per billion (still well below the Canadian drinking water standard of 100ppb). But Lenwood continues to be sick. Two weeks after my visit he was hospitalized again in Moncton for tests due to suspected pressure on the brain. Those tests showed no gross neurological damage, but Lenwood still suffers from headaches and his doctor is keeping him under close observation. Meanwhile, his father is looking for jobs out of the province.

"Working at the mill is like a marriage. You're punished for being unfaithful." That's the common attitude in Dalhousie, one millworker told me. The NBIP mill has been a good provider for the community, paying salaries of up to $30,000 to senior employees. But not all employees accept the company's practices without question. One of the dissenters is John McEwen, 40 years old, native to the north and proud of it: "You're sort of on your own up here, and of course it makes a better breed of people."

He has worked 22 years, all his adult life, at the NBIP mill and is currently serving a term as vice-president of the New Brunswick Federation of Labour. He is concerned about the clearcutting which the company has been practising for two decades in the drainage area of Southeast Upsalquitch, which is where the budworm epidemic was first detected. And he believes his concern about the future wood supply is shared by his fellow workers. "People here are not that removed from when we didn't do these things. We practised selective cutting when we had all sawmills. When you're a sawmill worker, you make damn sure you have a good tree next year. People know it's not being done properly now." He worries that real forest management will not be adopted in New Brunswick "as long as their mentality is entrenched in the 1940's perspective of things — you just go out and chuck something on the forest."

McEwen also has reservations about the spruce budworm spray program, not only because of health risks but because he believes it has failed even within the limited expectations of "crop protection." Defoliation is up 130 percent in New Brunswick (compared to a 50 percent drop in Nova Scotia where the epidemic has died). This could lead one to believe that spraying is ineffectual in curbing defoliation, which is the only government argument for keeping it. McEwen doesn't think his view makes him "unfaithful" to his industry: "I work in the paper mill. I want to continue to work there and I want it to continue to operate in the community. I think the one I work for is a good corporate citizen. But I want the wood supply to still be there. I'm convinced from what I've read and from talking to other people that there are better ways to manage a forest."

Maybe it was the melodramatic effect of driving around in the dark forests of New Brunswick, but I kept cycling on the classic image of Prometheus manacled to a mountain where nightly a vulture devoured his liver. Each day the liver regenerated and each

116

night the grisly vivisection was repeated. Spraying seems a similarly ugly forever proposition in New Brunswick. Hercules was finally able to unbind Prometheus from his mountain torture rack with a typically Herculean show of strength. It will take an equally forceful act of political will to unbind the budworm.

The consequences of not doing so are found in that man-made mountain of pulp in Dalhousie. The seemingly numberless logs spilling from the conveyer are in fact calculable. They are integers that can be slotted into the gross provincial product or the pulp and paper mills' year-end dividends or the bureaucrats' cost-benefit ratios. They are useful to those whom we hold accountable. The costs of the program to the environment and the human population are less amenable to empirical methods. They are so subtle it may take a long time for their numbers to come up. But when they do we may find ourselves powerless to express our collective loss.

V. THE OUTPOSTS

I am what the novelist Lawrence Durrell once characterized as an "islomaniac," that is, someone who has an irrational love of islands. I suppose there might be an ancestral reason for this affliction ("something in the blood"), for my mother's parents came from Cape Sable Island, or Stoney Island as it is more accurately called.

As an Atlantic Canadian chances are you'll discover "ghosts" — some part of yourself — if you push off for an island. At the general store on Big Tancook Island I chanced to meet an elderly relative, who, on learning my grandfather's name, reflected a moment, then said: "Jerry, yes, he was the one who drowned" — an event that had happened nearly 70 years ago, but one kept alive in memory on this offshore world.

On Tancook I was seeking the secret of its famous sauerkraut. I never did discover it, unless the secret is simply that there is pleasure and dignity in doing something the right way , an ethic I often heard repeated, in one fashion or another, on my travels to the outposts.

Islanders can be just a little conceited about the virtues of island life. Indeed there are many, but none is more cherished than the sense of freedom islands engender (which is strange when you consider that an island by definition is constricted). "You don't have no bosses to Grand Manan," 87-year-old raconteur, poet and boat designer Gleason Greene told me. "Grand Manan is an easy place to live. You can make a living easy, as far as that goes. You got no bosses; you don't have to run by the tick of the clock. You can.go where you want to go. Of course, you go on the tide when you're fishing. You go just the same, but nobody drives you. You go on your own."

Grand Manan is one of the last island kingdoms in the Atlantic realm. Our ancestors first settled these outposts to be close to the

118

fishing grounds. Now, in most cases, all that is left are stone cellars — and occasionally, sheep!

A peculiarly hardy breed of Atlantic sheep still roam the once inhabited islands of southwestern Nova Scotia. They thrive untended for most of the year and serve to remind us of the hardiness of the people who first settled this fog-wrapped, rocky coast.

Islands are also a place where dreams go to die. How true this is of Anticosti Island, that great juggernaut of limestone — bigger than Prince Edward Island — that juts into the Gulf of St. Lawrence. I had second thoughts about including this story, "The Land Of Lost Dreams," on an outpost of Quebec in a collection of stories about Atlantic Canada. But Anticosti is familiar, at least in name, to Atlantic Canadians as part of the lyrical triumvirate, "Chaleur-Miscou-and-Anticosti," of marine forecast fame. If I needed further justification, while there I learned that the first permanent settlers of Anticosti were Newfoundlanders and French Acadians from Baie de Chaleur. In the end, Anticosti is simply one of the most enchanted and haunted islands I have ever visited — with its emerald rivers, abandoned model towns, and its deer which have taken dominion over a turn-of-the-century millionaire's dream to erect a private Utopia.

One of the islands profiled here, in "Bottom Line," is not an island at all, or at least it no longer is. Georges Bank sank beneath the waves 7000 years ago, but for two centuries, this shallow "oceanic miracle" has been the haunt of fishermen from both sides of the 49th parallel. For a week I observed and shared in the work of the crew of the scallop dragger, *Adventurer II,* 100 miles out to sea from my hometown of Yarmouth, Nova Scotia. I have never seen men work harder — even in the mines. This is where the money is now in the fishery and so men doggedly, if not gladly, endure 18 workdays on a pitching deck. In the process of providing for their families they protect our sovereignty of the offshore.

It surprises me how nonchalant Canadians are about the vastness of their country; how sometimes they fail to see the necessity to have people on the land and on the water in order to speak, legitimately, of it as their own.

We sometimes forget that Atlantic Canada itself extends to the Arctic Circle. In northern Labrador I travelled north of Nain to Cut Throat Island where an Inuit family returns each summer to fish for salmon and Arctic char.

119

On this grey, ungiving rock, I gained an insight into the special relationship Inuit people have to the land, a forbidding land, and the iceberg-studded Labrador Sea which batters it. My host, Aba Kojak, explained: "It's hard to live on the Labrador. Always living off the land. That's our life — we eat seal meat, deer meat, birds, partridges, pigeon eggs..." Inuit have survived here — in "the land God gave to Cain," as Cartier so gratuitously called it — for millenia. Even so, they are now locked in a desperate battle with provincial and federal governments to gain access to the meagre resources they might well call their own. It seems an irony that we are reluctant to relinquish control of a land that we have so reviled, that we seem so determined to dispense the last dose of colonial justice to a people who have always been good stewards of the land.

Finally we come to Sable Island. It is one of the few places anywhere that man has failed to subdue; more often it is the island's treacherous shoals and confounding currents that have conquered ships and men, and thus earned this thin crescent of sand its grisly epithet, "Graveyard of the Atlantic."

Although the pall of its human history lifts only fleetingly, like the grey ceiling of an Atlantic sky, I found it a strangely peaceful place, a place where the natural order of things has reasserted itself. In the face of the elements and death, there is a surprising fecundity of grasses, seals, seabirds and horses. How long Sable will remain relatively inviolate will depend on our society's insatiable appetite for energy, as there is oil under the sands that have built this land where no land should be. Even as I write, there are companies gearing up, in an effort to extract it from beneath Sable's treacherous shoals.

OF CABBAGES AND KINGS

When the sauerkraut begins to smell,
  and it can't smell no smeller,
We take it from the barrel that's a-way
  down in the cellar,
We put him in the kettle, and it begins
  to boil,
So help me we can smell her round for
  40,000 mile.
—"Sauerkraut Song," from *Out of Old Nova Scotia Kitchens.*

"There used to be a lot of cabbage here on this Island once," says Calvin Hutt, his husky voice and burly frame filling the low-ceilinged kitchen. "My God, man, don't you talk. We used to have nothing under five or six hundred dozen. Some fellows would have a thousand dozen, twelve hundred dozen, and they all went to Halifax. Now, you see, there was one time, most of them was shipped to the West Indies on them big boats — lady boats, they used to call them, those white ocean liners. Now, when that was given up, it was only down to Halifax to sell them to the wholesalers."

On Big Tancook Island, at one time considered the sauerkraut capital of Nova Scotia, Hutt was once known as The Sauerkraut King. Now in his early 70s, he is old enough to remember the days when cabbage was the economic cornerstone of island life. The biggest heads were shipped on two-masted schooners to Halifax, a four hour trip with a good breeze behind you. The smaller cabbages were cut into kraut and packed in hundred pound half-barrels for export to the West Indies or for ready sale on mainland Nova Scotia. "Yes, we made lot of kraut," says Hutt. "One year we put in 500 half-barrels — used to hold about 10 gallons."

Hutt looks out the window at farm fields now gone back to alder and thistle, a grey scene made even bleaker by the low ceiling of grey Atlantic sky, and recalls a more pastoral season: "When we was making hay, we could hardly see each other, there was that much hay," he recalls. "We'd fill that barn up to where the swallows went in. Man dear, this used to be some place in the fall of the year, when the grass was taken off, and all the cattle was out on the land. Every fellow had his field fenced off, there was a lot of shareholders on this Island, good croppers. In the fall of the year, pretty near everyplace you went past some fellow was cuttin' in sauerkraut. Yeah, pretty near everybody who had any land at all, planted some cabbage."

In Nova Scotia, sauerkraut is generally associated with the South Shore, especially Lunenburg County, where German farmers were enticed in the early 1750s in order to feed the Cockney settlers and soldiers of the nearby garrison in Halifax. Among the staples the Germans supplied were cabbage, either fresh or in the fermented form of sauerkraut. Over the years, however, it became clear that the best sauerkraut did not come from the mainland but from a small island in Chester Basin — Big Tancook, one of 365 islands that stipple Mahone Bay. There are now fewer than a handful of cabbage growers and *Krautmeisters* on Big Tancook, but to sauerkraut lovers in Bluenose country, the Tancook name is still synonymous with quality. My purpose in coming to Tancook was to find out how Tancookers made their famous kraut.

Big Tancook Island, midway along the drowned coastline of Nova Scotia's South Shore, was first charted by the pioneer Atlantic cartographer, Joseph Frederick Wallet Des Barres, in 1760. He christened it Royal George in honour of his patron, George III. The island's first settlers, perhaps owing to their German ancestry or to a simple lack of pomposity, rejected this British appellation in favour of the Micmac name, Tancook, which means "facing the sea" — even though, from earliest days, Tancook Islanders did not look to the sea for their livelihood. In 1829 Thomas Chandler Haliburton noted that the residents of "The Great Tancook... derive their subsistence wholly from tilling the land." During the Age of Sail, Tancook did gain a measure of maritime renown for the design of the schooner-rigged Tancook whaler, a speedy and sturdy craft as well suited to racing as to fishing. But it was still farming, not fishing, that provided the island's principal occupation. It was not until the 20th century that the sea began to dominate Tancook life. Today, fishing for lobster, cod, mackerel and herring has brought a new prosperity to many Tancook households and, in the process, decline to the island's traditional sauerkraut industry.

"The younger people on Tancook today are earning five times the money fishing that they can earn cuttin' in sauerkraut," says Arthur Stevens, the retired captain of the Tancook ferry, who still cuts in a few tonne by hand every year for faithful mainland customers. "It's really not a money-making thing, but it's an art that you hate to drop. I've got a feeling that it won't be many years when there'll be none at all on Tancook."

Even the largest of the four remaining commercial Tancook *Krautmeisters*, John Cross, now considers kraut merely a sideline to his wage-earning job as a ferry deckhand. "There isn't money enough in it. I don't think if you counted your hours that you'd make $2.00 an hour at this." In 1985, Cross netted $2000 on his production of nearly six thousand pounds. Just a few years ago, Cross produced twice as much of his sought-after kraut, and 20 years ago, John's father used to keep a truck on the road peddling kraut under the E. & E. Cross label to the Halifax-Dartmouth area. Today, John's kraut is marketed by Hilchie Brothers in Chester, N.S. Most of it is sold in 5 to 30 pound buckets to general stores in eastern and northern Nova Scotia. "John makes real good kraut, his father did, too," says George Hilchie from his cramped waterfront office in Chester. "It comes up through the family." In the late 1940s, Hilchie's wholesale business moved more kraut than fish. Now the opposite is true. "It's a big dish but it's not as big as it used to be. Like you know, we used to sell a lot of salt herring and salt mackerel at one time. Now, the young people, two of them are working, got a microwave oven and they don't go into cooking herring or sauerkraut or stuff like that, and sales have dropped off from what they used to be years ago." Despite changing tastes, Hilchie can sell all the kraut Cross makes and then some. Cross ships his kraut aboard the steel-hulled ferry that daily services Big Tancook and its diminutive neighbour, Little Tancook. It docks in picturesque Chester Harbour and can carry freight and 150 passengers (nearly the entire population of the Islands). Chester has none of the practical demeanour of the nearby famous fishing port of Lunenburg. It is the most New Englandish of Maritime towns. Boutiques outnumber the stores, and most of the Cape Island fishing boats anchored in the harbour have been converted to pleasure craft and are anchored in the harbour alongside a flotilla of expensive and colourful sailing yachts.

The fare for the two-hour round trip from Chester to Big Tancook is $1. After we steamed out of the harbour, flanked by peninsulas that provide a prospect of the sea for oversize Cape Cod houses, neatly shuttered and trimmed, manicured lawns rolling primly toward the shore like giant welcome mats, I turned my attention to the ferry bulletin board. Cod nets were advertised for $75. Bingo night promised a $100 jackpot. There were the cards of two competing satellite dish dealers posted alongside a notice about the dance to be held at the Tancook Recreation Centre, featuring a group named for a locally famous schooner, *Nyanza*. We docked briefly at Little Tancook wharf, then shuttled over to Big Tancook, a collection of nearly flat-topped, straight up-and-down houses I have always admired for their wonderful simplicity. Our first glimpse of the island was like a child's drawing; the houses seemed drawn with a penchant for bright colours and clean lines. There were aqua clapboard houses with aqua fences, there were mustard houses, even robin's-egg-blue houses, built into a hillside that sloped toward the harbour. As bright as the houses were, they were less garish than some of the boats. Nestled side by side within the protective L-shape of the wharf were lavender, lime green and pink fishing boats. Obviously, here was a community unfettered by mainland conservatism.

On the wharf to greet me was John Cross, a short, smiling man in his early 40s, whose ancestors arrived on these shores more than a century before, bearing the surname Kraus and the Old World *Krautmeister's* secrets.

"What would you like to do?" he asked. "Maybe see the cabbage patch first."

In his black Ford pickup, we thundered over the pot-holed road toward the centre of the island. Three miles long and no more than a mile across at its widest point, Big Tancook is a comma-shaped islet that is perpetually sprinkled by Atlantic salt. Island vehicles hang onto their chassis by the thinnest of rusty threads. The corroded bodies flap like tattered rags as if they were going to lift into flight, and I guessed that there was not a muffler intact on the island nor a car that would pass a safety inspection. Like most islanders, John keeps a car on the mainland for highway driving and runs his truck on the 5 miles of island dirt road by whatever desperate means available.

We crested a hill and coasted to a stop at the bottom. John's half acre is the only sizeable cabbage patch on an island that a generation ago was boldly striped with fields of bulbous brassica. John's father also kept a dozen head of beef cattle; now there is not even a milk cow on the island and derelict trucks have replaced the oxcart. John has had to substitute commercial fertilizer for manure, although like his father, he still supplies organic content to his soil by collecting rock weed along the beach after winter storms. And despite islanders' abandonment of the land, many Tancook backyards boast at least a row of cabbage, enough to satisfy the undiminished island taste for freshly fermented kraut.

Although a late spring and too much rain in June, followed by an extremely dry summer, had conspired to stunt John's crop, there were some very handsome blue-green heads among his 5000 plants. And Tancook cabbages have long been noted for their exceptional size. Judge DesBrisay, island hopper and amateur horticulturist, remarked on two Tancook Brobdingnagians in his *History of Lunenburg County*: "In November, 1894, Mr. Sylvester Baker of the Island [Big Tancook] pulled two [cabbages] from his field, one of which weighted 25 1/2 pounds and the another 23 1/2 pounds."

On the mainland, 'Danish Baldhead' and 'April Green' are the favoured cabbage seed of commercial krautmeisters. On Tancook the cabbages have a homegrown pedigree."You might as well say that this is the old type of Tancook cabbage," John says, as he selects the largest heads, lops off the outer whorl of leaves and tosses the squeaky, 5-pound missiles unceremoniously into the back of his pickup. "It's not like any kind you're going to find in those seed houses."

John's cabbage is a peculiar Tancook hybrid. When he took over the sauerkraut-making duties from his father a decade ago, most commercial growers on the island had already gone out of business. Wisely, John rescued a couple of cabbage from each of the island's best kraut makers' kitchen gardens, planted these together in the small seed plot behind his bungalow and has used their cross-pollinated stock as a seed source ever since. John doesn't know just how far back into the mists of time the lineage of this Tancook variety of cabbage reaches. But it probably pre-dates his grandfather and may have its origin in cabbage seed that his German ancestors brought across the Atlantic in the 1750s.

John stores his cabbage with the roots intact in two of the last cabbage houses on the island. They are derelict though still serviceable structures, with fieldstone basements and eaves that touch the ground. The roofs were once double-boarded and filled with an insulating layer of sawdust but now the inside boards hang loose, and the roof is covered with eelgrass for insulation. On the coldest days, John installs a kerosene heater to prevent the cabbage from freezing.

In the spring, he selects a half dozen of the previous season's best heads and replants them. He scores the head with a deeply cut X, out of which bolts a six-foot seed stock. In the fall, he harvests the seed pods, and the Tancook cultivar is perpetuated for another season.

The Tancook hybrid is a late cabbage — planted the first of June it is not ready for harvest until mid-October or later — and perhaps the fame of Tancook kraut has something to do with its hand-me-down horticultural pedigree. Calvin Hutt thinks so: "See, we raised all late cabbage, where on 'the main' [Tancook for mainland] they raise mostly all early cabbage. There's a lot of difference between late and early cabbage for sauerkraut. Early cabbage isn't as good: it doesn't keep like the late kraut, it gets softer. Late cabbage stays better, firmer. We stuck to the late."

The excellence of Tancook kraut may also have something to do with the sure hands of the Tancook *Krautmeisters*, who seem to have practised a kind of legerdemain. Kraut making is as much an art as it is a science. I tried in vain to acquire a written recipe for Tancook sauerkraut, but none exists on the island. The right way to make kraut has been passed on from generation to generation, like the rhymes of a ballad, with no apparent need for a more permanent record of proportions or method. When there were many commercial kraut operations on the island, each maker's formula was a jealously guarded secret. With only four *Krautmeisters* left, the Tancook method is in jeopardy of becoming a lost legacy.

The ingredients could not be simpler: shredded cabbage, salt and water. There is no vinegar added to sauerkraut; the mixture makes its own "vinegar," actually lactic and ascorbic acid. This accounts for the sour tang and provides a good source of Vitamin

126

C, which recommended it as a scurvy cure in the days of sail. Just how sour the kraut gets depends upon the relative proportions of these ingredients and the ageing of the kraut. Tancook kraut is not very sour at all.

In John's kraut-making room — a garage-like addition to the back of his house — preparation begins with trimming the cabbage head. Using a filleting knife, John cuts off about an inch of the stump, then peels back the outer whorls of green leaf with quick flicks of the blade. He removes the outer leaves to get rid of any impurities — dirt, blemishes — but also for aesthetic reasons. "You get clear of the green," he says, "it makes a whiter sauerkraut."

He then splits the stump three times, so that it will shred more easily. Some makers core the stump out completely, but John thinks that the stump has a better, milder flavour than the cabbage itself. "That's just my opinion," he says.

The kraut makers term for grating is "cutting in." John cuts in between 500 and 1,000 pounds at a time. In the old days, all the cutting in was done by hand using a "kraut knife," a simple device consisting of a wooden base with two blades set in it like the blades of a wood plane. (One blade will suffice but will only cut the cabbage half as fast.) Two small rails running along the edge of this base provide a trackway for a bottomless box frame big enough to hold a good size cabbage head. The cabbage is shredded by being placed in the box and drawn back and forth over the blades. John's kraut knife was three feet long, a foot wide, and made of pitch pine. Now little more than a curious bit of Nova Scotiana, in its working days it cut countless tons of cabbage. Vincent Stevens, not a day under 70 himself, told me that in his prime he could cut in a ton a day by hand, and only the day before, he had cut in several hundred pounds. "It's hard work, hard on your back and your arms. It's all right when you're a young fellow but when you get up in years like I am..."

Today's large producers have opted for automatic cutters, albeit most of them homemade. John's father built the one John now uses. Powered by a small electric motor, the drive shaft is run off pulleys. The cutters are two scythe blades mounted on top of a vertical shaft like the blades of a propeller. A barrel top serves as a hopper, into which John feeds the cleaned heads, each head on its side to produce a longer, finer cut. "I try to get it as fine as possible," says John. The shredded cabbage falls into a bin, filling the garage with

127

the clean smell of coleslaw. With his motorized cutter, John can cut in a ton in an hour.

Although the colour and shred of the cabbage may be important aesthetic qualities, the step that follows cutting-in is ultimately more important to the taste of the finished product. John packs and salts his cabbage in huge wooden puncheons, the largest of which holds 1,000 pounds. John calls them "cherry barrels," but something more powerful than cherries may once have lined them, considering that Nova Scotia's South Shore was once as famed for rum running as for kraut making. He first applies melted paraffin wax to the inside of the barrel with a paintbrush — a sanitary measure, he says. Although the kraut is effectively sealed from contact with the wood, John maintains that "it gets a better flavour out of wooden barrels than say plastic or fibreglass." This has less to do with the kraut picking up flavour from the barrel than with the fact that wooden barrels maintain a more constant temperature, an important factor in the making of kraut — too much heat can cause spoilage, too little can retard fermentation.

John packs the cabbage in layers of four to six inches in depth, then compresses each layer by tapping it with a large maul. Some still use a wooden stamper that resembles the old fashioned butter churn. At one time, the cabbage was compressed by being stomped on with bare feet, like grapes. This may be more lore than historical fact but Tancook children, who still travel by ferry to high school in Chester, have to endure the mainlanders' sobriquet "Sauerkraut Stompers."

John sprinkles only a shallow handful of coarse salt on each layer of cabbage. "The more salt you put in it the more sour it'll get," he says. "You don't want to get it too sour." In search of the elusive recipe, I note that he uses about a handful of salt to every 50 pounds of cabbage. But this is not a hard-and-fast ratio either, as John points out. Depending on the time of the year, he uses more or less salt. For instance, he uses more in the fall when the weather is warmer, to retard the speed of fermentation, and less if it has been a particularly wet season and he wants to control the amount of brine the cabbage will make.

In John's opinion, the best type of salt was Turk's Island salt, but he can no longer get it. He now uses the same fishery coarse salt that island fishermen use to salt cod. He tried fine salt, but found it had a tendency to soften the cabbage because it dissolved more quickly. Salt keeps the kraut crisp by drawing juices from the cabbage — which is 90 percent water.

Left for 24 hours, salted cabbage will make its own brine. However, John prefers to add a little water after he has packed the barrel to the top in alternate layers of cabbage and salt. "I might use a little more water than some," says John. The more salt you put on the cabbage, the less water you will have to add, but also, the sourer the kraut: a delicate trade-off. John's goal is to avoid making the kraut either too salty or too sour. "I like something that you can take a bowl out and take a fork and sit down and just eat it raw," which is not the type of astringent kraut one remembers reluctantly eating as child. For cooking, John says, most people prefer a more sour kraut. As with maple syrup, it is a matter of taste: some people like strong-tasting, vinegary kraut, others prefer a lighter-tasting kraut. John adds five 3 1/2-gallon pails of water to a 500-pound batch of salted cabbage.

The last step is to cover the kraut and weigh it down to ensure that the cabbage is always immersed in the brine. John stretches clean plastic over the top of the puncheon, fits over it a piece of plywood cut to the inside dimension of the barrel, then weighs the cover down with a chest-sized, smooth beachstone — or "popple stone," as it is called on the island. The word (one of many in a rich local dialect) probably derives from the verb meaning "to heave — as in choppy sea." The sea washes the stone smooth as a plate, which is why John prefers it to rough granite that collects dirt. Mainlanders might not be able to duplicate his recipe without the popple stone, John jokes, but he adds that weighting the cabbage by some means is essential. The weight forces from the cabbage juices containing natural sugars that are the fuel of the fermenta-tion process. Also, the weight ensures that the cabbage remains immersed under the brine. If the cabbage were allowed to float to the top of the brine, it would probably become contaminated with yeast mould and turn an unappetizing "black and all the colours of the rainbow."

After salting and weighting, there is little to do until the cabbage is finished fermenting, usually in two to three weeks. John does check to see that his barrels aren't leaking, or that the powerful, gas-producing fermentation hasn't blown off one of the barrel hoops — not an uncommon occurrence, it seems. "That's why I've always got spare hooping around," he says.

Two weeks after my first visit, I returned to Tancook to sample John's kraut. The clean smell of coleslaw that had perfumed John's garage on my last visit had been replaced by a slightly illicit whiff of fermentation. I dipped out a handful of the finished sauerkraut, noting that its colour was the same as the freshly cut cabbage — a delicate white with a hint of pale yellow. Its taste had just the right tartness for my liking. This was the real thing, I thought; Tancook kraut, kraut without the "sauer."

"Good," I said. "It's not sour at all."

John smiled: "I think it's got a good flavour to it. It's not real strong. You could eat it whichever way you wanted to. You could cook it, you could eat it raw, some people fry it. You could use it much the same as a salad, like a coleslaw if you wanted to, whereas if it was real strong the only way you could eat it is if you cooked it."

Most islanders will tell you they prefer to eat their sauerkraut "ror" — raw, that is. If they do subject their delicate kraut to cooking, they simply boil it with corned beef. However they choose to eat it, it must be kraut made by Tancook *Krautmeisters* from cabbage grown on Tancook. They will brook no substitute.

When I went to the wharf to catch the ferry on Sunday, John was dressed for duty in his navy blue deckhand's uniform, transformed from *Krautmeister* to mariner as were so many Tancook Islanders before him. But as a newly-made mainland convert, I carried his secret in my right hand — a 30-pound bucket of Big Tancook Sauerkraut.

GRAND MANAN:THE GLORY AND THE GRIT

Grand Manan reveals itself only slowly. I did not so much as catch a glimpse of the island before the ferry *Lady Menane* nestled against the pylons of the berth at North Head, after our two-hour fog-bound passage from Black's Harbour, New Brunswick. Then the Bay of Fundy fog hung over the island in stubborn billows for the next week, enhancing the elusive character of this island which for most mainlanders is a place permanently shrouded in mystery.

For those better-acquainted with the island's virtues, it is a well-guarded secret. Year after year, for decades, painters and photographers have been drawn to the vistas of spruce-crowned capes receding into sea mist, the becalmed harbours bustling with boats, the wooden manors of 19th-century sea captains and the smokehouses poised on stilts above the Fundy tides. Generations of birders have found Grand Manan a place of wonder: even John James Audubon was impressed with the 275 species found there and did some of his sketches on the island. Latter-day naturalists come to see what may be the world's rarest whale, the North Atlantic right whale, which summers in the Bay of Fundy. Willa Cather, the great American novelist of the early 20th century, was so taken with the island's charm and quietude that she chose it as a spot to write many of her books. For all, it has been and remains a place to jettison the concerns of the mainstream, to be alone with nature and oneself, a true island of the spirit.

For some the qualities that set Grand Manan apart from "the main" are enough to qualify the island as a country of its own — and reason enough to make preserving the island way of life a common cause among Grand Mananers, born or naturalized. One of these proud island patriots is fisherman David Outhouse, who grew up on the other side of the Bay of Fundy at Tiverton, on Long Island. Owner of a herring seiner, he is often away fishing at night, but I caught him home relaxing during the day. In the driveway was a vintage, canary yellow Cadillac and in the yard was a flagpole flying an unfamiliar ensign: boat, lighthouse and maple leaf set off against a field of sea-blue.

"I had an idea always about wanting a Grand Manan flag," he explained. "I always figured Grand Manan was a special place, set off by itself. It's sort of a unique place."

He paused to reflect on his own meaning: "Well, it kind of rolls you back in time, maybe, when you come here. And I like it the way it is. I hate to see any changes in it. So I thought it would be nice if Grand Manan had its own flag."

Wedge-shaped in profile, the island kingdom of Grand Manan is 15 miles long and 7 miles wide. It is the largest of an archipelago of 20 islands straddling the Bay of Fundy and Gulf of Maine boundary. Passamaquoddy Indians from Maine simply called it *Mun-a-nook* or "island in the sea." Seven and one-half miles from West Quoddy Head, the easternmost point of the United States, and 22 miles from mainland New Brunswick, it is far enough from either shore for the people to have developed their own distinctive character and independence of political spirit. Descendants of United Empire Loyalists who settled the island in 1784, Grand Mananers do not think of themselves as just New Brunswickers. They are Islanders first. They are Canadians, to be sure, and proud of it, but with enough close family and business ties to Maine to render their speech most reminiscent of that of New Englanders. As one woman explained in the mellow tones one hears throughout the island: "Gen'ly, we ah a bit soft on the ahs."

But whatever else the alliance, to be an Islander is first and foremost to be allied to the sea. Disembarking from the ferry at North Head, visitors inevitably saunter down to the wharf to look over the fleet of seiners and longliners, trawlers and draggers, instinctively drawn close to that which makes the island tick. It was there, on my first trip to Grand Manan, that I met Floyd Brown, now 84, a retired lobster fisherman and weir owner. He is on the wharf most days, keeping track of the comings and goings, and he is generally willing to discuss Grand Manan's privileged place in the fisherman's universe.

132

"Around here, there's always something different," he said. "They go netting fish and line fishing — for cod, pollack, hake and haddock — and they got seiners and weirs, of course. Then there's lobster and scallops. And if you get right up against it, you can go clamming. There's lots of places they only got one thing. When it goes down, you're out of luck. Here, there's always something to go to."

The diversity of sea resources, fuelled by tidal upwellings at the mouth of the Bay of Fundy, makes Grand Manan a prosperous place by Maritime standards; there are few "poor-mouthing" fishermen to be found. Grand Manan is the only Maritime offshore island that has been able to maintain the population base it established in the 1880's when herring stocks boomed.

Like their ancestors before them, many Grand Mananers still fish with a primitive device called a weir, or "ware," as it is pronounced on Grand Manan. These heart-shaped pens, which at a distance look like gossamer colosseums, are connected to the shore by a long line of twine-strung poles called the fence. When the herring follow the flood tide inshore at night, they strike the weir fence and follow it offshore in an effort to go around the obstruction. Instead, the fence leads the school in through an infinite figure eight, the hooks of the enclosure constantly leading them back into its centre. The Islanders are proud of the weirs and name them as they might a boat: Sea Wall, The Dream, North Air.

Fishing by weir, explained Brown, "is the worst damn gamble you ever seen." Some years, he said, a weir may not "fish" at all; other years, the same weir may be full nearly every tide. It is then that the island's debts are paid off, new cars and boats are purchased and the kids get a holiday in Disneyland.

I once witnessed a big payday at one of the island's largest and most whimsically named weirs, The Mumps. Struggling against the racing tide, fishermen worked from dories to set a purse seine around the inside perimeter of the weir. That task completed, a rope strung through rings around the bottom of the net was drawn in, or pursed, thus enclosing the fish inside a giant bag. As the net was raised to the surface, the water under the boat turned a cloudy green. Millions of iridescent herring scales floated in the water like a galaxy of rhinestones. Six fishermen clutched the net's cotton mesh with white-knuckled determination and leaned their collective weight into raising the bounty of fish. As the tide and teeming fish slowly yielded to man and machine, the scene before me — viewed from the seine skiff's cabin roof — seemed to invoke an inexplicable legerdemain: the sea was drying up. Instead of water, there were fish, a seething, electrifying mass of herring. Those on the surface, suddenly finding themselves out of their element, flapped desperately against one another, beating the scales from their silver bodies in a death throe that created a milky plume which steadily expanded toward the perimeter of the weir. One of the fishermen, pausing in his labours, glanced up at me and said, "Isn't it a pretty sight when they dance like that? It makes them scale better when they dance too."

Before the day was over, I had watched 250,000 pounds of herring pumped from The Mumps, a haul worth $23,000 to the weir's five partners.

The small herring were destined for a sardine factory in Maine. In the 19th century, before the canning process was developed, small fish were either discarded or used as fertilizer or a source of oil. Large herring were preferred for the burgeoning smoked herring trade in Europe and West Indies. In 1884, 18 million pounds of smoked herring were shipped from Grand Manan, making it the world's largest producer. While the market for smoked herring lasted, the half dozen small villages that hug the low-lying eastern shore of the island enjoyed unusual prosperity.

A century later, many of the weathered smokehouses perched above the water in Woodwards Cove serve only as billboards for adolescent graffiti. But puffs of pungent smoke have been issuing from under the roof caps of more and more smokehouses in recent years, promising a partial revival, if not a full-fledged return, of the industry that was once the cornerstone of the island's economy.

Hovey Russell, one of those anticipating a turn in the fortunes of smoked herring, has reopened some of the smokehouses in which he learned the arcane art from his father. An alchemical essence — earth, air, fire and water — emanates from the dark doors of Russell's buildings. A hundred years old, their very timbers are preserved in herring oil.

"Smells good, doesn't it?" a worker remarked as he went about his morning routine of laying fires. Half-cured herring hung above him, tier upon tier, in amber legions that seemed to glow with their own light, like the smoky chimneys of thousands of low-burning lamps.

The fire builder made small piles of kindling, slab wood and sawdust on the gravel floor. With a shot of oil and the touch of a torch, the fires blazed up momentarily, then died down to begin their daylong smouldering.

Russell, now in his sixties, learned how to smoke herring at the age of 13. "The fire has to burn low, no blaze to it whatsoever. You can burn them too. You have to watch what you're doing, all right," he said, indicating the brine tanks where the herring are salted before being strung on pointed sticks for hanging in the smokehouse.

"If all goes right, the finished product is ready for eating in a month. You take them home and boil them with some new potatoes, you got something good to eat."

Not everyone agrees with Russell. The taste for smoked herring, as for all salted foods, has declined in recent decades in North America. Inflation has ravaged the traditional Caribbean markets. Last year, three-quarters of a million pounds were produced, a paltry amount compared with that of a century ago but reason enough for Russell's optimism about the prospects for a resurgence of the grand old industry.

"I think it's really picking up because we've had people from New York and different places, and they want to know when the herring's going to be done. The same people was here last year."

People return to Grand Manan with the alacrity of pilgrims. To most, life on the island seems governed by a less insistent clock than that of the hurly-burly world left behind. However, according to Eric Allaby, local historian and harbour master, the belief is simply not true: "One of the illusions of the place, of course, is that the life of the fisherman is pretty laissez-faire and easygoing. But, in actual fact, what seems like a very easygoing kind of timetable is ordered by the tides or the wind or the weather — it's just a different set of rules than what the more artificial parts of society live by." Allaby's remark itself reveals a common Grand Manan conceit: life on the island is the real thing, while mainland existence is, at best, a pale imitation.

My own initiation into the strictness of the tide as alarm clock came my first morning on Grand Manan. It was 4 a.m. and still dark when I rolled from the comfort of my bed, intent on catching the early tide at Dark Harbour. Surrounded on three sides by cliffs and bounded at its mouth by a great seawall of beach stone and drift wood, the salt lagoon is the only safe anchorage on the west side of the island. In sharp contrast to the sheltered coves and gentle marshes of the eastern shore, the west coast, with vertical cliffs of basalt rising 200 to 400 feet from the sea, is an ironbound nightmare to mariners. Dramatic as its name, Dark Harbour is a seasonal home to dulse pickers and cottagers, and its sole connection to the sea is a narrow channel that was dug during the 19th century and is negotiable only at high tide.

I was going dulsing. Grand Manan is particularly noted for its dulse, a red seaweed that grows luxuriantly on the island's rocky coast. In 1984, the island exported 125 tonnes. Rich in vitamins and minerals, much of the dulse goes to health-food stores. It is used to flavour soups and stews. But many people — Islanders especially — like to eat the seaweed as a salty snack, fresh from the sea, sun-dried or cooked on the stovetop. Dulse grows all around Grand Manan, but to Leroy Flagg, one of my companions that morning and the island's best-known dulse buyer, there is only one dulse worth picking: Dark Harbour dulse. The high cliffs, he says, shade the dulse grounds at their base, preventing the rockweed from getting sunburned. Also, the strong tidal currents on the west side of the island seem to favour the growth of the dulse while keeping it clean of mussels and mud.

It was a Sunday morning, and the highest tides of the month, the so-called dulse tides, were past. Perhaps that was why only a handful of drowsy dulsers had shown up, rather than the dozens that set out regularly to pick between the tides. Perhaps, too, the poor turnout had something to do with the dance at the curling club the night before.

After cautiously winching Flagg's Lunenburg-built dory up and over the protective seawall's crest, we launched ourselves into the pearl-grey waters of the outer Bay of Fundy. We cut a clean wake through a mysterious void of dense fog and grey sea. Only the ephemeral weirs — ghostly houses for air and water — gave relief to the seascape.

We put ashore in the shadow of the cliffs to the north of Dark Harbour, where we found a good patch of foot-long dulse. I marvelled at Flagg's knack of knowing where to bring us despite the fog that was almost thick enough to obscure the towering coastline.

"You can't fool me on the dulse," said Flagg. "I know every rock and curve on the coast. I suppose I've picked over every rock 5,000 times. I can always find good dulse because I can keep it in my mind. I know where we picked six or eight weeks ago."

Flagg's right arm was in a cast and sling, but he set about picking with his good hand, displaying the same unharnessed enthusiasm he has had for the task since he was 12 years old. "I like the sound of dulse; I like that snap." Clutching a mittful of ruddy, glistening Dark Harbour dulse, he held it up proudly: "This here is the only dulse in the world."

Handful after handful pulled away with ease. A good picker can gather enough dulse to yield 100 pounds after it is sun-dried on a field of beach stone. Flagg pays pickers $1.75 per pound for the finished product. We had two hours between the tide's uncovering the dulse rocks and covering them again, and the rhythm of the picking made the time pass quickly. We loaded our half-dozen 50-pound burlap bags into the dory and sliced our way home through the fog.

Ironically, it was the fog, a most unlikely quarry, that the first summer people came in search of. Before the advent of air conditioning, fog was considered just the palliative for hot sticky nights. Droves of the well-to-do flocked to the seaside hotels that lent an air of Old World gentility to the Eastern Seaboard.

Today, most of these resorts are in shambles. One survivor of the bygone era of steamer trunks and straw boaters was the Marathon Inn which rises above the tiny fishing community of North Head like a haughty dowager. In 1977 it was 100 years old and in a sorry state of disrepair. It was then that Jim and Judy Leslie of Toronto answered an ad for the sale of the Marathon. The Leslies eagerly took possession and set out to restore the down-at-the-heels Inn to its former glory. They hoped to capitalize on what Jim describes as the island's "escape aspect," a perennial attraction to urbanites. In creating an ambience to match their renovations, the Leslies decided to offer beer, wine and spirits with their meals, and they took the seemingly innocuous step of applying for a liquor licence. In doing so, the Leslies ran afoul of the Islanders' deeply held conviction that Grand Manan should stay the way it has been or once was.

It was the surprise beginning of a long, hard battle for the Leslies and a resounding introduction to the gritty determination of their new neighbours. Grand Mananers, it seemed, had done without a drinking establishment in the past, and they were not about to have one now. Many residents were still bitter about the opening of Grand Manan's single liquor store, which they felt was not only contributing to the deterioration of island morality but also creating a safety hazard along the island's single stretch of road. Clutching Bibles and babies, the teetotalling congregations of Grand Manan's Ministerial Association, counting among themselves more than 800 of Grand Manan's 2,600 souls, made a pilgrimage of protest to the Provincial Legislature in Fredericton each time the Leslies submitted a new application. Until 1984, when the license was finally granted, the Leslies' application, and concomitant mass exodus to Fredericton, was an annual event. While most of the arguments posed by the Islanders were both moralistic and pragmatic, many also contained a sentiment that perhaps lay even closer to the heart of the matter. "I'm not against tourists," one Islander grumbled, "but I'm against changing things around to suit them." Another, ruddy with anger, was even more succinct: "We don't like change on the island."

Such resistance runs deep in Grand Manan. No sooner had Grand Mananers lost their battle with the Marathon Inn than the island's citizens mounted a campaign against another threat to the island's status quo. Panic rippled through the community when it was learned that Moonies — followers of the Reverend Sun Myung Moon's Unification Church — had purchased two of the island's lobster pounds to supply church retail outlets in the eastern United States. The Grand Manan Ministerial Association, representing the island's 17 churches, was harshly critical of the Moonies' avowed motives. "The Moonies are so two-faced at times that it put fear into me," said Reverend Wayne Robertson of the Central Wesleyan Church. "They're not here just to buy and sell lobsters. They must have come to Grand Manan to further the Unification Church."

To an outsider, it might seem that one more church would make little difference — already there is one church for every mile of road. One explanation for the God-fearing nature of the people is offered by Daniel McGee, pastor of the Emmanuel Pentecostal Assembly: "I guess fishermen see how humble they are in the scheme of things because of the elements. Every day on the water, they see the awesomeness of creation."

Apparently, awe and humility have yet to breed religious tolerance. Ronald Benson, a lobster-pound owner and fish processor, echoed the island sentiment: "Most of the concern is the Unification Church as such, not the business aspect of it. This is the main concern of the citizens of the island, that we not lose any of our young people, or anyone, to that cult."

Although the Moonies have not yet proved to be a threat to local fish buyers, most Islanders remain vigilant. One Mananer who seems nonplussed by the commotion is Buddy McLaughlin, who sold the lobster pounds to the Moonies. McLaughlin does not appear to be worried about being censured by his fellow Islanders. "I've got broad shoulders," he says offhandedly. Neither does he share the view that island-owned fish operations would not be able to compete with Moonie-run enterprises. He puts his faith in his own shrewd business sense — another island trait, judging by local prosperity. "We've bought and sold these particular pounds three times now," he says, then adds wryly, "each time at a profit."

Though the wider world sometimes impinges on this sea-girt kingdom, for the most part irksome mainland issues can be ignored or regarded at a comfortable, even smug, distance. After being on the island for a while, a visitor begins to believe what everyone has been saying: Grand Manan is a place apart, not only in setting but also in spirit. Islanders enjoy the independence that isolation breeds. "They don't have no bosses to Grand Manan," said Gleason Greene, an 87-year-old raconteur and former boat designer. "Grand Manan is an easy place to live. You can make a living easy, as far as that goes. You got no bosses; you don't have to run by the tick of the clock. You can go where you want to go. Of course, you go on the tide when you're fishing. You go just the same, but nobody drives you. You go on your own."

For many, the ease that Grand Manan engenders is something they grow into and come back to renew. Some enquire about real estate; others are so hard-bitten by Grand Manan's version of "islomania" that they stay — despite themselves. Robin and Mary Wall, for example, knew the first time they set foot on the island that they wanted to make Grand Manan their home.

In his mid-fifties, Wall left his longtime post as art teacher at a community college in Cornwall, Ontario, where, he admits, he and his wife had been perfectly content. On Grand Manan, they cleared away alders, designed and built a printmaking studio and joined

139

the church and historical society — all within a year. They are now firmly rooted.

"What the hell is it about this island that attracts so much?" Wall puzzled as he showed me his prints of weirs, smokehouses and rocky shores that reflect his artistic conversion to the island's iconography.

Mary, who now works as the island's first school psychologist, immediately began to answer his question, making an extemporaneous list of island virtues. It evokes childhood — not one's own, she pointed out, but the state of mind. There is also the neighbourliness of the people: the Walls have opened their door to find anonymous gifts of illicit gulls' eggs — "Delicious," they confess — or a string of stream-caught trout. And when they were building, neighbours dropped by to ask if they needed anything and to pitch in.

Wall listened, nodding. "You know, it just doesn't feel like Canada here. It's as if I'm in my own country. I like that...." He paused, looking at the print in his hand, and I silently finished the thought for him, the thought that would complete his transformation from mainlander to Islander: "And I'll work to keep it that way."

ISLAND PASTORAL

Tasha, a seven-year-old border collie, is balanced with her front paws on the gunnels of the *Bar-Tender* , a Cape Islander fishing boat, as we approach the rocky shore of McNutts Island at the mouth of Shelburne Harbour. Though we are still too far from shore for me to distinguish sheep from the bulks of grey granite boulders, Tasha obviously can smell them as she thrusts her nose eagerly upward, sniffing the sea air. Ranger, an older sheep dog with a black spot around one eye that looks like a pirate's eye patch, joins Tasha at her lookout. These two 'salty dogs' are all anticipation, eager to get ashore and on with the task at hand — to round up the sheep which roam wild on McNutt's Island off Nova Scotia's south-western shore.

Islands are scattered like pieces of a jigsaw puzzle along the deeply indented coastline. Sheep have been kept on many of them for more than a century. Romantic theories abound as to how they got there. It is said that sheep were placed on some islands to provision shipwrecked sailors; on others the first sheep may have been survivors of shipwrecks. A more plausible version of events is offered by a Dr. J.F. Ellis in his turn-of-the century report, *The Sheep Industry on the Atlantic Coast of Nova Scotia.*

"In the early days when the horse was a novelty in this region and public highways were little used, the fisherman's only means of travel was his boat," he wrote. "Consequently a great many of them lived on these islands. But of late years they have nearly all moved to the mainland, and at present only a very few of the islands have any inhabitants. However, the sheep, left on these islands by the old inhabitants, thrive and do well..."

In this century, the practice of keeping sheep on islands was carried on by fishermen-farmers who occupied the islands seasonally for lobster fishing or the gathering of Irish moss, a

141

commercial seaweed. As late as 1960 there were 8,000 sheep on islands from Canso on Nova Scotia's eastern Atlantic shore to Brier Island in the outer Bay of Fundy. Often several owners — in some cases, descendants of the original island inhabitants — managed the sheep co-operatively, and shearing time became an occasion for a big picnic, a kind of island reunion.

The number of island sheep has since dwindled to 2,000 (following a general downturn in the sheep industry), and flocks are restricted to 30 islands in southwestern Nova Scotia. A handful of island sheep owners persist in the time-honoured practise there because sheep seem to thrive despite the harsh offshore environment, and often it proves more profitable than intensive management on the mainland.

Walter Perry of Central Chebogue, Yarmouth County, runs the largest island sheep-farming operation in the province. As I drove into the farm yard, three border collies circled about the car to greet me, and soon their master emerged from the white farmhouse with a welcoming hand extended. At 77 Perry is a vigorous man with bushy black eyebrows, a shock of white hair and ruddy complexion. He showed me into his kitchen where he had spread out on the table maps of the coast showing *his* islands — Mud, Seal, McNutt's and Emerald Islands, among others.

Perry bought his first purebred flock of sheep in 1932. "I guess I was born to have sheep," he said with a smile, "because I like them, and I always seemed to have pretty good luck with them." As a boy he had helped a local farmer raise lambs on Crawley's Island at the mouth of the Chebogue River, but Perry did not get into island sheep for himself until the 1950s, when a Cape Negro Island sheep owner offered him his flock at a price he could not refuse. He now has 700 ewes on eight islands, in addition to 125 at his mainland farm which borders the tidal Chebogue River.

Traditionally, island sheep were raised primarily for their wool. "I think the women used to be more interested in the sheep years ago," said Perry. "They did their own spinning and knitting mittens. Quite often you'd find the women were doing more shearing than the men, who were probably out fishing when women were doing the farmwork."

In the past, the transportation of lambs to market was a practical constraint, whereas wool could be processed locally or stored and shipped in any season. As barren ewes, rams or wethers (castrated males) will give double the wool clip of a pregnant or lactating ewe, they were often retained to the detriment of the lamb crop, which today is the key to success in the sheep business.

Like most contemporary sheep producers, Perry was more interested in maximizing the lamb crop than the wool harvest. To increase lamb production, he saw that the island flocks had to be managed more carefully. It was therefore vital to remove rams in the summer months and return them in early winter so that ewes would lamb in late spring, thereby increasing chances of survival for the lambs. This meant more trips to the islands rather than the once-a-year shearing frolic.

That was fine by Perry. "There's a challenge and a pleasure there that's hard to describe," he said. "A walk around any island is a pleasure, I think. There's always something different to be seen. I guess there's some beachcomber in me, too." Sadly for Perry, a heart attack two years ago has kept him ashore, and he now leaves the beachcombing and the round-ups to his two sons, Tom and Ron.

When Tom and Ron Perry arrived at the wharf in Gunning Cove on a balmy evening in mid-July, the captain of the *Bar-Tender,* Clifford Van Buskirk, quipped, "Time to leave off fishing and go sheeping." Van Buskirk was accompanied by his brother, Dwight, their 13-year-old nephew, Randy, and Randy's friend. Clifford, one of 11 children of the former McNutt's Island lightkeeper, is now a full-time fisherman but continues to keep sheep, a hobby that began when the Perrys gave him a pet lamb.

After the hour-long run out Shelburne Harbour, Van Buskirk steered his boat around the north end of the 20-square-kilometre island where we put over a punt into the water. Heads of curious harbour seals poked above the swells as we rowed ashore, leaped onto the slippery rocks and scrambled to higher ground. McNutt's was named after a notorious 18th-century character, Colonel Alexander McNutt, who settled on the island in the 1760s after an attempt to found a Utopian colony, New Jerusalem, at what is now Shelburne. In her book, *Offshore Islands of Nova Scotia and New Brunswick,* author Allison Mitcham notes: "Islands such as McNutt's were not... so easily tamed as their early inhabitants hoped. McNutt's has always defied the incursions of civilization." And so it is today.

We followed a narrow sheep path through the thick tangle of underbrush which grows to the edge of the island's splash zone.

Telltale wisps of wool clung here and there, but it was not until we arrived at the lighthouse grounds that sheep came into view. This so-called lighthouse flock moved off warily and we split into three groups to encircle them and drive them to the beach. We would later be joined by another sheep farmer, Elizabeth Hyde, and helpers to gather the three flocks on the island.

"This is the most fun for us," Ron Perry said as we picked our way through boggy ground to the rocky shore. "Just to see if you can do it. It's a challenge. It gets in your blood after a while."

Part of the challenge for us on this evening was to get the job done before nightfall. On a wooded island such as McNutt's it is best to drive sheep in the evening, Ronnie explained, for it is only then that the sheep come to the shore from the woods where they seek shade during the heat of the day. In the woods, they are nearly impossible to find or retrieve.

The sheep threaded between the deserted lighthouse outbuildings in obedient file. I was surprised by the orderly progress of the flock, and asked whether island sheep were in fact "wild" when compared to mainland flocks. "They're not so much wild," Ron said. "I'd say they're foxy, they're cautious."

As if to affirm his observation, a small group of ewes and lambs suddenly bolted. "They're going for the woods, better send the dog out," Ron shouted, and the "king dog," Ranger, followed in hot pursuit. It was a quarter of an hour before he reemerged at the heels of the errant sheep. One panicky ewe headed for the water where Dwight Van Buskirk had to administer a football tackle to keep the animal from plunging into the waves.

"If sheep get pressured too much, they get suicidal, and they'll even drown themselves," Tom Perry explained. "I've had to go for a swim more than once.

"Let her rest," he urged. This proved the most dramatic episode in the four-hour hike which took us halfway around the island. The sun set in a vivid display on the western shore, and the evening star rose through a salmon-coloured sky. Soon we had only our flashlights to show us the way as we stumbled on behind the sheep, lulled by the anxious bleating of the lambs and the deeper maternal calls of the ewes.

I overheard two boys holding counsel in the dark. "It's like in an old Western movie," one said. I took his meaning, as one reinforced by the terms *roundup* and *drive*. However, what we were doing is formally called a *gather*, which, I thought to myself, would find its closest analogy in the outer islands of Scotland. By the time we reached our shearing corral, the tide was high, forcing us to ford a shallow creek. With a little encouragement, the flock passively crossed over into the makeshift corral.

After six hours sleep, we were up again to do another sweep of the island in an attempt to gather the sheep we had let pass through our human net, or others that had fallen by the wayside. Among the latter were the "swaybacks." It was easy to pick out these lambs from the flock — their hind quarters sway back and forth uncontrollably, making it next to impossible for them to walk without stumbling. The partial paralysis is caused by a demylenization of the spinal cord and is attributable to copper deficiency in the diet.

Swayback is endemic to some islands and not others. McNutt's has a high incidence — up to 20 per cent of lambs may be affected — but even on McNutts there is a variation between the "lighthouse flock" and the "pen flock" at the other end of the island, which is almost free of swayback. According to Mac Fuller, Agriculture Representative for Shelburne and Yarmouth counties in southwestern Nova Scotia, swayback on the island may be related to a gull colony at the lighthouse and its influence on the vegetation. Fertilized by a steady application of bird droppings, the rich vegetation in the area may be depleting the soil of copper. Longtime sheep farmers have commonly associated swayback with the presence of seagulls, much to the scepticism of professionals at the Nova Scotia Department of Agriculture. But farmers may have a valid point, said Fuller. Another factor may be sandy soil types which are often copper deficient. Acid rain, a major problem in the region, may also be affecting what little copper there is present in island soils.

For the past several years, the Department has funded a program to prevent swayback; it encourages farmers and veterinarians to inject liquid copper into ewes in the last trimester of pregnancy. However, success of the program depends on the ability to land on the wind-battered islands in March — a risky business at best.

Wintering on the islands — some of which are bald and lack shelter — is perhaps the greatest threat to the flocks. Elizabeth Hyde, who owns the largest flock on McNutt's and is its only year-round resident, knows well the perils sheep face in winter. The cold winter affects them more than a heavy snowfall, she said. "They seem to know where the hay is and they'll dig away at the snow with their hooves." Inevitably, however, there are losses.

As we talked, we spelled each other in carrying a swayback lamb to reunite it with its mother at the shearing corral. We came across evidence of last winter's severity in the carcasses of ewes and lambs; there were also old orange lichen-encrusted bones of the generations of island sheep that had lived and died there. Up ahead were the survivors, wending along the shoreline and reminding us that life goes on.

Until 50 years ago, little new stock was introduced to the islands. The sheep were described as having distinctive deer-like faces and probably were descendants of sheep from the British Isles. Common breeds such as Scottish Blackface, Suffolk and Cheviot have since been mixed in, but island flocks remain characteristically robust. "Mother Nature does the culling," says Yarmouth veterinarian Tommy O'Brien. "As a result they tend to develop a hardier breed than on shore."

O'Brien has treated island sheep since 1978."Production of island sheep is good, and in some cases higher than on shore," he noted. "It's amazing the body condition these animals will have. Even after lambing they will have high body fat." He attributes the good conditioning of ewes to the virtues of kelp, their primary winter forage. Kelp has a high protein content, essential amino acids, and a salt balance close to that of the body. Because it is naturally salted, the inherent food value is preserved. "It is as good a wintering feed as you can find," said O'Brien. "Provided there is enough kelp being brought ashore by good winds, they'll do well."

Several years ago, the population of common green sea urchin, which feed upon kelp, exploded along the Atlantic seaboard and, as a result, greater sheep mortalities were experienced on some offshore islands. It underlined how sheep depend on land and sea for nourishment, and how these two ecosystems are intimately connected in this offshore world. Sheep feed primarily on kelp from October to May, then switch to forage inland. "They eat bayberry bushes, it flavours them; wild roses, it flavours them; wild mint," Elizabeth Hyde observed. "They're the best tasting lamb in the world."

Ann Priest, an actor and part-time sheep farmer helping Elizabeth Hyde that day, guided her dog, Tess, with whistles, hand signals and soft-spoken words. Tess, in turn, did an admirable job of bringing the stray sheep to the corral where the shearing began mid-morning and proceeded all day. I watched with amazement as professional shearer Bill Oulton cut the fleece from a sheep in 90 seconds flat. I tried my hand, upending a ewe and clamping her between my knees. She showed remarkable patience with my novice effort, but half way through decided she had had enough and made her escape. Tom Perry, who could not contain his amusement, finished my ragged job.

The sheep were treated for parasites and vaccinated against tetanus. The tagged ewes were checked to see if they were lactating, and the lamb crop divided up among the three flock owners.

By the end of the day we had sheared 120 sheep, and everybody, weary from the two roundups and hot work, found a soft bag of wool to rest on as sandwiches were eaten. "To me it's more like a picnic, though after the twentieth sheep I start wondering how many more there are," Tom Perry remarked. "I always enjoy the community aspect of it." I asked Randy Van Buskirk, who was nursing a sore knee that had been butted by a rambunctious ram, what he thought of his first island sheep shearing. "It's fun," he replied, adding with enthusiasm. "And tomorrow they dock the tails!"

On this trip, all lambs would have their tails clipped, male lambs would be castrated, and mature rams removed to a nearby island. (Several South Shore islands bear the name Ram Island, probably because they were used to segregate the rams from the flock during the summer.) In September and October, island sheep owners will return to pick up their market lambs, leaving 10 per cent of the ewes to maintain flock numbers. Again in December, they brave high seas and bad weather to return the rams to the islands. "You take your life into your hands to make a landing in a small boat," Walter Perry had said before we set out on our trip. "You've got to have a good man on the oars and another man with the ram in the stern of the boat. And before she touches the ground, that ram's got to get out of there and up over the beach, and you've got to be ready to get rowing out before the next roller hits you. I've done that a good many times."

The risks inherent to island sheep farming are balanced by greater profitability. On islands there are no fencing or feed costs as the sea acts as fence and forage provider. There are fewer predators on islands than on the mainland, although last year two island flocks were decimated by coyotes that swam from the mainland. Raising island sheep requires less work because the animals do not have to be tended every day. However, the cost of transportation to and from the islands offsets some of the gains. I concluded that to undertake this offshore adventure one must not only love sheep but islands too. It was well past dark before the *Bar-Tender* pointed its bow toward Gunning Cove. Clifford Van Buskirk was going home to the mainland, and then to sea again to fish. "It gives me an excuse to go out around the lighthouse twice a year," he said, reflecting upon his island sheep enterprise.

His statement struck a responsive chord. I realized that in Nova Scotia island sheep rearing is not simply a business but a carry-over of a vanishing maritime culture. Now that nearly all lighthouses have become automated and the communities that sustained island families are no more than cellar holes and memories, island sheep help keep that historical offshore connection alive, for Van Buskirk and other Nova Scotians too.

LAND OF LOST DREAMS

Henri Menier had turned the French predilection for chocolate into a fortune of 200,000 million francs by the time he was thirty-five and, as the Chocolate King of France, could well afford the dream of owning his own island. He required that the island should have a good harbour for his three-masted, 800-tonne barque and that it be able to support his passion for "a life of sport and adventure" with rod and gun. In 1895, after much searching he learned of just such a place, an island in Canada called Anticosti that was shaped like Madagascar, was one-quarter as big as Belgium and protruded like a great Juggernaut at the mouth of the St. Lawrence River. What interested Menier was Anticosti's largely unsettled state, its teeming game and, especially, its famed salmon rivers. The asking price was $125,000.

Menier immediately dispatched his good friend Georges Martin-Zede, a journalist of independent means, to assess prospects first hand. After inspecting the island's crystalline salmon rivers, wooded interior and two small communities, and after making a circumnavigation of the island's 580-kilometre, Dover-white limestone coast, Martin-Zede recorded his enthusiastic reaction in his journal: "I had set out with the thought of finding a preserve for fishing and hunting. I returned with the very decided opinion that this island was susceptible of a development such that I would be willing to give all my time to it. The island was too enormous to be made a mere summer residence. Unquestionably, sooner or later, we should engage in colonization."

Menier's imagination was fired by Martin-Zede's report, so much so that he authored a grand plan for his new acquisition. Over the next 30 years, the Menier family was to pour $5 million into the Island. Under Martin-Zede, a model settlement named Baie-Ste-Claire was created, a network of roads and railways constructed, a small fleet of ships launched, a lavish 30-room Norman/Nordic-style villa built for Menier's personal use and a veritable bestiary — white-tailed deer, moose, beaver, reindeer, buffalo and even frogs — imported.

Today, the Menier name lives on in the island's only settlement, Port Menier. Baie Ste. Claire is now a ghost village facing Quebec's bleak North Shore, and the Menier villa has long since disappeared, razed by fire in 1953. Ironically, the most conspicuous sign of the short-lived Menier rule of Anticosti is the white-tailed deer. Of all the Menier experiments, the introduction of deer was the most successful; today Anticosti boasts the highest density of deer in Canada, ten to the square kilometre. I soon grew accustomed to seeing deer wherever I went on the island, and quickly learned the islanders' reflex of standing on the truck's brakes to avoid a collision on the dirt roads which thread the still unpopulated interior. The deer, which fellow sportsmen Menier and Martin-Zede would certainly have enjoyed in their fashion, stand as a kind of rebuke to their civilizing tendencies. But then Anticosti has steadfastly resisted all of man's best-laid plans to call it his own.

Last summer, intrigued by the island's history, I decided to become one of the handful of tourists that annually visit Anticosti. To this day, the island is best known as a destination for privileged hunters and fishermen but as the small plane lifted off from Sept-Iles on Quebec's North Shore, I also wondered what other surprises the mysterious island had in store.

The townscape of Port Menier, a village of 300, is distinguished from the more modern boom towns of Quebec's North Shore by touches of antique architectural grandeur. High-pitched mansard roofs, gables and fanciful cupolas figure the horizon. Cupolas adorn the otherwise drab green civic building that, predictably, houses the essential services — a post office and Caisse Populaire — and, most unexpectedly, a lingerie boutique. There is an epicerie where, as befits a one-community island, all staples from bread to beer can be found, and local novelties, such as whole fox furs from the island's traplines, are on display.

I stayed in one of the Swiss-chalet style row houses, built at the turn of the century for Port Menier workers. The *Maison du Cap Blanc,* as the name suggests, provides a view of a limestone headland, but also of an uncommonly long wharf, which for most of my

150

stay was cowled in silence. Once a week, however, Port Menier erupts with a communal honking of horns as a public announcement of the ferry's arrival. Half the community, it seems, turns out to greet a returning family member, receive a parcel or, like myself, simply share in the excitement. Then, just as suddenly, Port Menier slips back into its repose.

My first foray into the unpopulated interior of the Island was to the Jupiter River, a famous crystal-clear fisherman's dream that cuts deep canyons through 50 miles of Anticosti's soft limestone. I was accompanied by Michel Asselin, director of island operations for the Quebec Crown Corporation, Societe des etablissements de plein air du Quebec (SEPAQ). The province purchased the island in 1974 with the intent of creating a provincial park but soon found that it was too isolated to attract much of the general tourist trade. The government fell back on Anticosti's hunting and fishing appeal, and today the island is leased to SEPAQ and several private outfitters in a renewed effort to make the sports industries profitable. The price of an Anticosti hunting or fishing trip is at a premium. SEPAQ charges from $1000 to $2600 for a five-day fishing package on its better rivers.

The best river — indeed "the best river in the world," according to Asselin — is the Jupiter. When Menier owned the island, he kept the Jupiter strictly for himself and his retinue. They anchored Menier's yacht off the river mouth, and then horses, wading in the chill water to their chests, pulled the pampered anglers upriver on canopied "Cleopatra's barges." Governor General Lord Grey, an avid salmon angler, was Menier's first guest at the opening of his villa in 1911, and a photograph survives showing the two smoking cigars as they are pulled up the river.

Today, the major pools are accessible by dirt road, but they are still the destination of an elite. "Everybody from Prime Ministers to the richest man in the U.S., take your choice," says Asselin. His pick-up descended through primevally thick softwoods, and suddenly, there it was: an emerald ribbon flowing over a riverbed half-exposed by low water and so intensely white, it made me squint. Downriver several hundred yards, two deer waded across a shallow narrows. From the verandah of the log cabin lodge of Jupiter 12 (so named because it is 12 miles upriver) I laid eyes on what must be, if not the best, then certainly as beautiful a salmon pool as exists anywhere.

The waters of the Jupiter are gin-clear. But where they deepen over white limestone ledges, the colour turns to an exquisite shade of pale jade. The pool skirts a 20-meter cliff of sedimentary limestone that rises like a geological wedding cake on the shore facing the lodge. Salmon lie there, perfectly visible and apparently doubled in the jewelled water, as their shadows are thrown onto the river bottom. Looking down at the pool, I understood the sentiments of Jupiter 12 chief guide Fernand Bujold, who, at 37, is a 16-year veteran of his profession."It's pretty easy when you work in Paradise," he said, gesturing to the river and woods. "Fish all over the place, and deer all over the place. It is easy to learn your job."

Later, as we jolted back toward Port Menier over the ridged limestone roads, Asselin spoke enthusiastically about SEPAQ's plans to expand their services to tourists as well as hunters and fishermen, the longtime devotees of Anticosti. "If we open up the island they will come. This is the last frontier. There is no pollution, and there are wildlife for them to see everywhere. The whole island is like a zoo. All the animals that are here, you see them. With time and investment, it will become tourist Paradise."

I could not disagree with Asselin's assessment of the island as an unspoiled preserve. With no effort at all, I saw countless deer; silver, red and black foxes; moose; owls; eiders ... the list goes on and on. However, I did come to ponder the term "paradise," thinking how consistently it was used to describe the island, both in historical accounts and contemporary conversation. It became apparent that there was a paradoxical hitch in the outsider's thinking about the island: of starting with a natural paradise and then, through elaborate man-made plans, turning it into something even better. The history of Anticosti is of grand schemes and dreams that briefly flowered on its shores, then withered, leaving the island's implacable forest and its ironbound coast to reassert their primacy.

Of all the islands of the Gulf — the Magdalens, St. Pierre and Miquelon, Prince Edward Island — Anticosti was the most resistant to European settlement. It was long visited by Montagnais Indians who canoed the 20 miles from Quebec's North Shore. They called the island Nasticousti, which means "hunting ground of the bear." Jacques Cartier circumnavigated two-thirds of its coast on his voyage of discovery around the gulf in 1534. But except for its use as a seasonal anchorage by European fishermen, the great island, which is a quarter again as big as the province of Prince Edward Island, was ignored as a place of settlement until the mid-17th century.

Its first settler was a remarkable man named Louis Jolliet, who counted among his many accomplishments the exploration of the Mississippi River, for which the Sun King granted him the seigneury of Anticosti. After the death of Jolliet's son, Anticosti again reverted to an utterly wild state for another century and a half. It seemed that no one wanted Anticosti, even nominally. Newfoundland and Quebec shunted their claims back and forth until finally Quebec assumed legal ownership in 1825.

In spite of its checkered public history, Anticosti has held a strong attraction for colourful individuals, beginning with Jolliet and certainly including Menier. But no denizen of Anticosti has ever matched the notoriety of Louis Olivier Gamache. A resident of the island until his death in 1854, Gamache was known as the Wizard of Anticosti, and, in the local lore of the gulf, was invoked as the devil incarnate. He was widely held to be responsible for luring ships to their demise by posting false beacons along Anticosti's shallow, dangerous shores. Gamache's ghoulish reputation seems to have been largely undeserved, but Anticosti's epithet as "Graveyard of the Gulf" certainly was not.

Anticosti's limestone shoals, ghostly and fatally deceptive, stretch out for three kilometres beneath the waters of the Gulf. "The dangerous, desolate shores of Anticosti, rich in wrecks, accursed in human suffering. This hideous wilderness has been the grave of hundreds, by the slowest and ghastliest of deaths — starvation...," wrote Sir James Le Moine in Chronicles of the St. Lawrence. The morbid truth of his words was borne out by the October 1825 wreck of the *Granicus*. Survivors faced winter with no food and minimal shelter. In the spring, unsuspecting sailors found only the gruesome evidence of rampant cannibalism.

If the treachery of Anticosti's waters was indisputable, the potential of its land to nurture a colony remained a matter of speculation throughout the 19th century. Despite a report that the soil was "in general shallow and incapable of raising farm crops," the dream persisted that Anticosti, like Prince Edward Island, could be turned into another Garden of the Gulf. In 1884 a London entrepreneur, Francis William Stockwell, set about selling Anticosti's dubious virtues to his unsuspecting countrymen in a pamphlet entitled "The Settler and Sportsman in Anticosti." When his venture folded five years later, the stage was set for Menier's arrival upon Anticosti's shores.

At the time, there were two permanent communities at either end of the island, one settled by Newfoundlanders, the other by Acadian French from Baie de Chaleur. Menier's grand plan called for the creation of what amounted to a feudal estate, and when the Newfoundland residents of Fox Bay resisted, they were evicted as "undesirables." The Acadian community of L'Anse aux Fraises continued, though under Menier proprietorship, and Martin-Zede began planning the community of Baie-Ste.-Claire, at the northwestern tip of the island. Menier was in many respects generous toward his loyal charges, providing free schooling and the first medicare plan in Canada. The model farms, sawmills and lobster canneries provided employment for all willing to submit to the authoritarian Martin-Zede.

One Anticostian who remembers when Menier was the law is Florrie MacCormick, a handsome, ageless woman who wears the island life well — a few years ago, she shot the largest buck during the island's annual fall hunt. A third-generation Anticostian, she had one grandfather who hailed from Newfoundland and another from Baie de Chaleur. She recalls that when she was a child, a warden prevented anyone, even children, from picking wild strawberries and fishing for trout near the Menier villa. Nor could people go into the bush without a permit. Although the Meniers treated people well, she says, after the company came there was more freedom. "You had more places to go. If you wanted to go into the bush, you could."

The company Florrie was referring to was Anticosti Corporation, a pulp-and-paper consortium that bought the island from the Meniers in 1926. McCormick's husband, Charlie MacCormick, was the island's best-regarded guide until his death in 1982, but originally, he was one of 1000 lumberjacks who came to Anticosti to work for the company during the island's brief logging boom. Anticosti's 500,000 acres of spruce and fir was then the largest standing reserve of pulpwood on a newsprint-hungry continent. At Port Menier, which possessed the island's only navigable harbour, the longest wharf in Canada was built. As a visiting American writer observed in 1927: "There's something gigantic under way in Anticosti."

154

But, as had happened before, the grand plan, put into practise, came up short. The Depression closed down operations, and the loggers fled back to the mainland. Charlie MacCormick, lured by the rivers and bush, was one of the few who stayed. At the behest of the pulp company, he pioneered commercial guiding for the American "sports," an endeavour that became the basis for the island's cash economy. As sole owner of the island, Anticosti Corporation, like Menier before them, felt a paternalistic responsibility to provide as best they could for residents, even though pulp operations did not resume until 1947. Thereafter, logging continued until 1974 when the Quebec government purchased the island for $10 an acre, or nearly $24 million — in what was one of the largest real estate transactions in Canadian history. For the first time in three centuries, since Jolliet was first granted the seigneury, Anticosti was public domain. It was no longer anyone's personal paradise.

As if its separation from the mainland had ordained as much, Anticosti has always had a destiny separate from the rest of Canada. It is no longer a park, although the provincial wildlife service still strictly controls hunting and fishing on the island, nor is it a province, though by sheer dint of geography, it might qualify as such. And, because of its isolation, it is solidly unilingually Francophone. I found, however, that residents were willing to polish up their English (which, some confessed, they had not spoken in several years) in a good-hearted effort to communicate their passion for *l'Anticosti.*

There was some irony in their accommodation, for my visit coincided with the celebration of St. Jean Baptiste Day, Quebec's national holiday. The party began as the sun set over Quebec's North Shore, and the youth of Anticosti began to gather at Pop's Bar on the outskirts of Port Menier. Mid-evening, the insistent thumping of North American rock was replaced by more lyrical Quebecois *chansons*, and the dancers and drinkers in the dingy bar began to gravitate outside, where they sat sipping beer and staring passively into a large bonfire that exhaled spirals of sparks into the starlit night. To an Anglophone mainlander, it seemed not so much a nationalistic celebration as a simple pagan impulse of the young to herald summer. But later, local passions welled up in conversation around the bar.

"Anticosti is *fantastique*," said Gilbert Blaney, who occupied the stool next to mine around the circular, vinyl-padded bar. "It is not just a salmon or a buck. You know, I was born here and I am sorry the people just come here for fishing and hunting. If you can look right, you'll see a lot of things."

To the sports, whether they are well-heeled Americans in pursuit of the king of sports fish or Quebecois, of which nearly 5,000 come every fall for the virtual assurance of returning with a bag limit of two deer, Anticosti remains just that — a salmon and a buck. But from those who have stayed longer, I learned of the island's more subtle virtues.

My host on the island was one of those not-so-transient Anticostians. Gaetan "Alex" Laprise has been a wildlife-management technician with the Quebec Ministere du Loisir, de la Chasse et de la Peche on the island for three years. As we feasted on a meal of sea trout which he had caught that morning on the Becs Scie River, one of Anticosti's more modest but still productive rivers, he spoke of his growing contentment, "It all depends on what you want. If you want cinema, restaurants, theatre, it is not good. But if you want skiing, clean snow, quiet, then this is the place to be." By consensus winter is Anticosti's best season. After the sports have gone home, the guides have time to spend at their own camps in the interior, lake-fishing, trapping or snowmobiling. "Almost nobody works, it is like a holiday," says Laprise.

But best of all, it seems, in all seasons, is to be a child of Anticosti. Sister Benigna Lord, who came to Anticosti from Madagascar three years ago, soon realized that the children of this, her new island, were very different from the children of the island she had left behind. "When I came here three years ago, I said they were 'free like the deer.' I wasn't used to it. I came from Africa where the children are quiet and keep their head down. But here, they are very excitable. I said to myself, 'What kind of deers are these?'"

Sister Benigna is the only sister on the island, and when the planes cannot land because of bad weather, she conducts Mass or, as happened last winter, a funeral in the priest's absence. When I first met her she was sitting in the kitchen of the parish surrounded by five shy children sucking on her home-made popsicles. "All the children think I'm lonesome," she joked. "All the day long they come here."

There are now only 41 children in the island's school, and they must leave in their early teens for the North Shore to attend high school. When they return, Sister Benigna sees the influence of the mainland: "When they come back here, they are different. When they are here they are outside all the time, they are free to go everywhere. It is not the same spirit when they come back. At 17, they say, 'There is nothing to do here.'"

What to do, not so much for leisure but for a career, is a pressing problem for the youth of Anticosti who wish to stay on their island home. The largely seasonal jobs revolve around "the sports" and are limited to guiding, mechanic, cook and camp showboy. Even these positions are not as assured as they once were, as outfitters frequently recruit guides from the Gaspe and North Shore and, in recent years, have reduced the number of employees in cost-cutting efforts. Raymond Bond, the principal of St. Joseph School, admits: "I'm trying to make the students understand, if they want to do something interesting, they have to go and live outside. I tell them in order to do what you like to do, you must think of leaving."

Bond, an 11-year resident of the island, has also grappled with the problem of alternative employment for Anticostians as the first mayor of what is Quebec's newest municipality. From Menier's rule to the Quebec purchase in the mid-1970s, there has been a complete economic dependency on a single employer and therefore little entrepreneurial spirit. One of the ironies of Anticosti-life is that there are no commercial saltwater fishermen on the island. Surrounded by water rich in fish and frequented by boats from other parts of the gulf, Anticostians themselves have never turned to the sea for a living. The only non-sport fishermen I saw on Anticosti were the "lobster pickers" who drive their trucks onto the ebb-tide exposed shoals illicitly to pick the crustaceans for their own stewing pots. Bond and others have lobbied for a fish processing facility but the high cost of diesel-generated electricity and distance from market have so far discouraged developers. Recently, there has been talk of reviving pulp cutting to supply mills on the mainland, but the prospect worries some wildlife biologists who believe clear-cutting would negatively affect the deer population. As one resident wildlife technician pragmatically observed: "No deer, no Anticosti."

George MacCormick is the only one of Charlie and Florrie MacCormick's six children now living on the island. He considers himself to be one of a lost generation of Anticostians, who left the island in the early 1970s during the pull-out of Consolidated-Bathurst. He, alone among his contemporaries, returned to the island a decade later "to appreciate what I had when I was young." Currently, MacCormick is superintendent of Quebec Hydro's generating station. He admits that his commitment to staying on the island only extends to the day when his own children will have to leave to finish their schooling. Many Anticosti children, denied a family setting in Sept-Iles, drop out. MacCormick is determined to better chances for his own children even if it means abandoning his beloved-Anticosti. Contemplation of that prospect seems to make the native son philosophical: "Menier tried a lot of things. My father used to say, 'If you want to do something on the island, read what Menier did, and then try to do something else."

Not since the demise of Baie Ste. Claire have people attempted farming on the island, and even logging, begun by Menier, may never return. The best bet for the Anticosti economy seems to be diversification of tourism that is now based solely on deer and salmon. SEPAQ is actively pursuing an alternative tourist trade. Pascal Samson, an environmental consultant, has been hired to survey the island's flora and fauna with the goal of developing nature tours. Samson first came to Anticosti to investigate the caves (some of the largest in Quebec) which have been carved by the percolation of water through the island's soft limestone. The same soft limestones have yielded splendours like Vaureal Falls, which is higher than Niagara. As a geological relic of a sea that covered the area 60 million years ago, Anticosti is littered with marine fossils and today, its basic soils support an unusual, acid-rain-resistant flora, including 19 species of orchid.

As we slogged through a bog in search of the rarest specimen, *Orchis rotundifolia*, Samson spoke of the type of person who might be attracted by Anticosti's natural wonders: "I want an ecological tourist, someone interested in ornithology, speleology, fossils. I'm not interested in the tourist with shorts, flowers on his shirt and photographic equipment hanging around his neck — not a tourist from Old Orchard Beach. I want a very special tourist." I wondered how far and wide he would have to look for such people. Samson himself seemed to be one of those rare persons who appreciated Anticosti in its unembellished natural splendour and who did not want to change it to suit themselves.

Later, when I pondered Menier's efforts to turn Anticosti into his private paradise, I remembered the evening I accompanied island warden Paul Grenier on his nightly look-out for deer poachers, who make their raids by boat from the North Shore. We drove the few miles from Port Menier through wind-stunted spruce to Baie-Ste.-Claire. As the sun set over the gulf it threw a golden light across the old farm fields of the ghost village. A herd of some 40 white-tailed deer roamed across the area once encompassed by Martin-Zede's zealous vision of a prosperous colony. Two abandoned buildings were all that remained of the short-lived experiment. "It was a big village here and they built it for just a few years," said Grenier with a dramatic sweep of his arm. "Now, look. Deer and wild meadows." The legacy of the chocolate king.

BOTTOM LINE

Captain Gary Frost stands at the centre of the shiny varnished wheelhouse, pondering an impressive array of marine gadgetry: four Lorans, two radar and an old fashioned brass magnetic compass mounted in front of the wheel. The scene beyond the nine bridge windows — a green-grey, undulating expanse of moody ocean flecked with dainty storm petrels — could be anywhere in the nondescript North Atlantic, but as Frost's checkings and cross-checkings confirmed, we were on Georges Bank, 160 kilometres southwest of Yarmouth, Nova Scotia, and a scant 5 kilometres from the newly drawn, and uneasily maintained, boundary line that defines the limits of Canada's jurisdiction over the richest fishing bank in the northern hemisphere.

Our position was critical, for Frost's 36-metre wooden scallop dragger, *Adventurer II*, was steaming full throttle toward the line, towing two 14-foot-wide scallop drags along the sea bottom, as we have been almost constantly since our depth sounder signaled our arrival on the shallows of Georges twenty-four hours before. Frost was keen to work as close to the line as possible, yet to cross it would mean the loss of his boat and the end of his career — at the age of 35. The same fate awaited the captain's counterparts from the United States but as Frost was quick to point out, the threat has not always proved a deterrent: "This is where a lot of the activity has been. Now it's all shells." By "activity" Frost meant American scallop boats running the boundary line to scoop up Canadian scallops.

Frost is a confident man who loves his boat and the Bank, and he likes to talk about both. I shipped aboard the *Adventurer II* primarily to learn about scallop fishing but soon discovered that one does not fish on Georges Bank these days without also learning about politics and confrontation. "Couple months ago," Frost recalled, "there were three or four Americans across the line in the nighttime; and then one guy got brazen around 9 o'clock in the morning and came across."

This illegal activity continues two years after the International Court of Justice in The Hague handed down its binding decision on the marine boundary dispute in the Gulf of Maine. Canada had claimed less than half of Georges Bank, while the United States had petitioned for complete control of Georges based on what it argued was historical dominance of the region. After hearing 9600 pages of testimony, the International Court of Justice made the predictable politic decision, splitting the claims down the middle. Canada was granted one-sixth of the bank, a 35 by 70 mile section known as the Northeast Peak. Reaction in Canada varied from "disastrous" to ecstatic," but no one denied that the decision gave to Canada the best part of the scallop ground and important groundfish spawning areas. Historically, the Northeast Peak has yielded 60 per cent of the total Canadian and American scallop catch, and hence American skippers are tempted to cross into Canadian territory despite the risk of heavy fines and the threat of confiscation of their million-dollar vessels.

An independent breed, accustomed to roaming the Bank at will, fishermen of both nationalities must now exercise restraint, and many are finding it difficult. Traditionally, Canadian fishermen exploited Georges side by side with Americans, and many regarded each other as friends. One Canadian scalloper I spoke with considered the Americans as "almost like family." There is truth in his sentiment, for the eastern United States and Nova Scotia have exchanged goods, services and personalities, as well as fishing grounds, for two centuries.

Georges Bank sticks out like an upturned thumb between Massachusett's Cape Cod and Nova Scotia's Cape Sable. For more than a century it has been a favoured fishing hole of people from both sides of the Gulf of Maine, and prior to the 1977 claims by Canada and the United States to a 200-mile limit, it was the haunt of foreign fleets as well. One Russian trawler captain remarked that Georges Bank was nothing less than "an oceanic miracle." All the oceanographic criteria are met to nurture marine organisms. The Bank is shallow — as recently as the last Ice Age it was an emergent island — thus, well shot with the sunlight necessary for photosynthetic production. Furthermore, as part of the Gulf of Maine-Bay of Fundy system, Georges is subject to strong tidal action, which results in vertical mixing of seafloor nutrients. The presence of nutrients tumbling through light translates as biological productivity; at Georges Bank, however, the combination has resulted in a productivity estimated to be four times that of the legendary Grand Banks. Its nurturing capacity is obvious even to the casual observer. In my few days on the Bank, at any given time I might see whales feeding or shark fins knifing the waves and, always, hundreds of seabirds skimming the waters — all signs of the fishy riches lurking below the bleak surface, which billows and falls like the roof of an enormous big top.

In the northern hemisphere Georges is an unmatched fish producer. In 1985, Canadian landings of all species from Georges were worth $52.7 million at the wharf. Of that total, the scallop fishery was by far the most valuable, bringing in $39.5 million. Lobsters added $1.6 million, and groundfish such as cod and haddock made up the balance of $11.6. Georges Bank alone accounted for more than one third of the total Nova Scotia fishery and generated an estimated 3600 jobs.

Obviously, the high-stakes scallop fishery is not taken lightly by men like Frost. He reminded me that there are 15 wives and maybe 75 or 80 kids counting on him and his boat. For that reason Frost is attentive not only to his own approach to the line, but to any transgressions by Americans. Squinting into the radar screen Frost saw six amber blips, a mile and a half into the American side. Although we cannot yet see them through the fog, Frost knew that they were American scallop draggers, and in his mind, there was no doubt that they were simply biding their time, waiting for the right conditions to cross the line and plunder *his* scallops. "They just stay on their side of the line, and when the weather gets right for them to take a jump, maybe the six of them will come at once."

The right weather would be southwest winds and more fog, exactly what the marine forecast had been calling for all day. At the moment, however, the fog was lifting ever so slightly, and to starboard we could just begin to make out the silhouettes of two big stern trawlers, National Sea Products' boats out of Lunenburg, dragging the Banks for groundfish. Frost trained his binoculars to the "nord," where he picked up a third vessel on the horizon.

"That's our coast guard. I know it, I know it, I know it." He handed over the binoculars just in time for me to see the long grey vessel swing round and begin plowing water in our direction. Frost whooped with laughter, exhilarated by the mock chase. "He thinks we're Americans trying to sneak back across the line, or if we're Canadians, he wants to tell us we're getting too handy to the line." Frost swivelled and grabbed the radio behind him: "Fisheries Patrol Boat *Cygnus*, Fisheries Patrol Boat, *Cygnus*, this is the *Adventurer II*. O'er." Then turning to me Frost said, "If they're playing cat and mouse with the American boats he might not come back."The game of cat-and-mouse has been played almost non-stop since the line was drawn. There have been 44 reported incursions into Canadian territory since January 1985. Eighteen of the offending boats have been brought into Nova Scotian ports and given fines from $25,000 to $45,000 plus the loss of their catch. In the opinion of many Canadian skippers, Gary Frost among them, the only measure that will eventually put a stop to the violations is for the Department to seize a boat.

"That's what you gotta do, you got to make the fine so steep, that it won't even enter your mind to cross the line. See, now when you catch them, seize the boat, and put a couple hundred thousand dollar fine — that would stop it, in my opinion. But when you're given a $30,000 fine, and there's fifteen guys chippin' in on it, it doesn't do much, you see. If you get 4000 pounds of scallops a day, they're gettin' five bucks a pound, that's $20,000 right there. And it's amongst 15 guys, like I said, that's the way they're doing it. Now these six guys we seen might be all buddies, right? And they might have it all lined up. They left the dock, and they said, 'Look, we're goin' close to the line, and if we get caught, whoever gets caught, whatever the fine, we'll split it.' You see, now, that's the way they usually do it."

In January 1987, Frost and others got a portion of what they have been pressing for, when Canada announced a substantial increase in the maximum fine — from $100,000 to $750,000. In the past the Department of Fisheries and Oceans has requested from the court confiscation of the offending vessels — albeit unsuccessfully — and it will continue to do so whenever it thinks the abuse warrants it.

Ultimately, the stakes are so high that perhaps there can be no certain deterrent. Some American captains feel that they have to take the chance of running the line to keep a crew and make payments on their vessel. Even the possibility of losing their vessel

163

may not dissuade them in the end. According to one DFO official, "A lot of them say, 'Take my boat, the bank owns it anyway.'"

Access to Georges Bank has been equally critical. Many believe a line drawn more favourably for the United States would have meant not only financial ruin for a few fishermen but economic ruin for the whole region of Southwestern Nova Scotia. Since the mid-1800s, fishermen from more than 30 small ports along a 320-kilometre stretch of Nova Scotia coastline have been sailing what was originally called St. Georges Bank. First, they put to sea in saltbank schooners searching for cod, and then later in modern steam trawlers in pursuit of halibut, haddock and swordfish. The scallop fishery did not begin until 1945, but it quickly assumed prominence after Captain John Beck returned from an exploratory trip to Georges with 8000 pounds of "deep sea scallops," the Georges Bank mollusk that many seafood connoisseurs consider a delicacy second to none. Word spread along the coast, and the next year, boats began gearing up for Georges. By the mid-1960s Canada dominated the scallop fishery on the Bank, with 50 offshore draggers working the Northeast Peak and Northern Edge — the tip of the thumb to which they were pretty much limited by distance from port.

It is a 12-hour trip from Yarmouth, home port of the *Adventurer II*, to Georges Bank, and as I was to learn during my days on board, those in-transit hours are the only ones in stints of up to a week when the crew of 14, the captain and mate are not frantically working to "make their trip" of 26,000 pounds.

"You can't lose time in this," explains Frost. "It ain't like any other fishing. It's average, the fishing's got to go on a solid average, you don't get a big day. If I get 3500 to 4000 pounds a day, I'm well satisfied."

We rode a fog swell all the way out, Frost vehemently and alliteratively cursing the fog for the entire distance. The depth sounder indicated our arrival on the Bank. "She comes up pretty quick," said Frost, referring to the shallowing water. At dusk the veil of fog lifted long enough for us to see that three other scallopers were on the Bank — "Lady boats," belonging to Comeau Seafoods of Meteghan, northeast of Yarmouth.

Turning on the radio as we wallowed in grey hills of water, Frost tuned in to hear someone's thoughts about their lawn back home: "I think I'll try some Kentucky bluegrass — it's nice and green."

Frost cut in to ask what the scallops were like, and the voice came back with barely a change of tone: "Meat's gone out of them — o'er." Frost, though, was anxious to get a few scallops in the hold, after checking the depth — 90 fathoms — he gave a blast of the horn, the signal for the crew to "shoot away."

"We'll take some here," he said, "then we'll look around for better bottom." The book on Frost is that he's a real dog for new bottom. "He'll find scallops where nobody else can find them," I was told. The winch cable sang through gallows' blocks. Frost let out a length of "wire" equal to three times the depth plus ten fathoms for good measure. This ratio (the same as that used by fish trawlers) usually settles the two-tonne rake on the seabed. Frost went slowly until the rake was in position, then he gave the boat throttle. Each tow is three and a half to four kilometers and takes about twenty minutes.

The rake looks and functions like a giant dustpan. As it is towed along the bottom, scallops and other bottom-dwelling creatures, rocks and trash, are swept into the net of chain-mail and rope. It is an unsubtle device, and for every scallop caught, another is probably crushed by the rake's rambunctious passage.

The horn sounded again, and the deckhands and winchmen moved into the waist of the boat to receive the rake. They did so with an unsettling nonchalance, considering what they were grappling with. Three men worked each side. Two deckhands attached boom hooks to the rake, turned it and then cleared the deck while the winchman, who operates the boom cable from a safer position below the wheelhouse, brought the rake crashing nose first onto the deck. Scurrying across the tossing deck once again, the deckhands detached and repositioned hooks so that the winchman could upend the rake, spilling its contents onto the dump tables.

The emptying of the rake is a continual fascination, for one can never be sure what will appear from the nets. Scallops, of course — pink, white or brown, plain or patterned, large and small — but also, if the beds being dragged are old ones, as many half shells as live scallops. And with the scallops comes the rest of the benthic marine ecosystem, as well as a portion of the sea bottom itself in the form of sizable boulders.

I soon become familiar with a rogue's gallery of sea-bottom monsters: yellow and orange spotted deep sea skates, conger eels that are half fish, half pouting look-alikes for Mick Jagger, and, without exception, monkfish — perhaps the ugliest members of this menagerie. They vary in size from a half meter to more than a meter in length, most of which is head — a spiny, abhorrent visage, wide as it is long, bisected by an enormous mouthful of tiny razor sharp teeth. The relatively insignificant tails, called "monkey-tails" by the fishermen, are delicious, I was told, and much sought after by Japanese buyers. If there are few scallops to be had, the monkey-tails are iced away. As well, there are nondescript creatures like "sea-pumpkins," which I at first mistook for blobs of oil. One day, there was the rare catch of a manta ray, a creature that must be lovely in the water gliding on its sea wings but on deck looked like a collapsed mass of grape jelly. One of the deckhands posed with it and then unceremoniously kicked it through the scuppers.

For their part, the fishermen ignore the zoological curiosities, with which they are all too familiar and which make their task of picking scallops more difficult. Legs spread, head between their knees, my shipmates bent to their task of sorting through the trash, flipping scallops into plastic baskets with lightning speed as they sorted through the marine trash. Once I got my sealegs, I picked for a few hours each day. "Good job for a strong back and weak mind," said one of my fellow pickers. It's also hard on the hands: it's common to go through a pair of heavy rubber gloves every two days.

Once the tow had been sorted through, Frost again sounded the horn. The dump tables were lifted, depositing the trash back into the sea, and then gently returned to the deck. A crewman appeared and as the boat listed to his side, he cracked the handcuff holding the rake with a maul, and it plunged once again toward the riches of Georges Bank.

Shoot away, drag for twenty minutes, haul up, dump the contents of the drag on deck, and shoot away again, a never-ending frantic cycle in the quest to return to port with 11,800 kilograms of fresh deep-sea scallops.

Frost is a driver. In 1985 he caught more scallops than any other captain in southwestern Nova Scotia's Sweeney Fisheries fleet. He went to sea at age 11 and had his Captain's ticket by 21 and the command of a scallop boat at 24. He is anything but a fairweather Captain: when the other boats have headed for home, Frost is still fishing."I wish you could be here when it's blowing 50 or 60," said a longtime crew member. "I tell everyone to clear the deck until the gear stops flying."

While there might be occasion for grumbling in the forecastle, the crew of the *Adventurer II* fares better than most of their counterparts, and that is compensation enough. In 1985, the *Adventurer II*'s crew share was twice as much as that for many boats. As well, the crew respects Frost's willingness to shed the trappings of rank. "He won't ask you to do anything he won't do. He doesn't stay in the wheelhouse and yell at you, he gets down on the deck and picks just like you. You don't see that in too many boats."

Frost has steel rods in both legs, the result of his putting a car up a tree at age 19, and the rods seem to inspire respect from those who work with him. By the time he's 50, doctors have told him, he will be in a wheel chair. Now, though, several times a day, he leaves the therapeutic comfort of his $1100 captain's chair, shouts an obscene salutation from the bridge, then bolts for the deck to start picking.

The scallops are whisked to the shucking room. In fact, it is not a room at all but a cramped corridor on either side of the galley and the aft cabins. There, every scallop — by my reckoning 750,000 on our trip — must be handled once again. The men stand at a long steel trough, rocking heel to toe in a kinetic trance. Each has his own customized kitchen knife, ground, curved, tapered and taped to his liking, that allows him to work at top speed. The knife is inserted between the two halves of the scallop, and one flip of the wrist ejects the bottom shell and viscera out a facing open bay — to the delight of the greater and sooty shearwaters ("hags" to fishermen) who follow the boat faithfully. Another flip of the wrist scrapes the remaining shell clean, and the scallop meat — the muscle — falls into a stainless steel pail. A fast worker can fill a bucket an hour. On the first trip of the year, the men frequently get "shuckers wrist," an inflammation that swells their forearms to twice their normal size. I could keep at it for an hour at a time before my wrist began to give out — not to mention my back and legs.

I admired my shipmates' stamina. There was a constant clacking of knife against shell like the sound of castanets or musical spoons. In my bunk, with a porthole that looked into the shucking room, I went to sleep and woke up listening to the cacophony. When they are into scallops, as they were then, the men work double

167

shifts, knowing that the sooner they make quota, the sooner they will go home. That means eight-hour watches, with just four hours to sleep and eat before starting again. "We'll go right out for a week now, no stops, 16 hours a day," said crewman Dave Reid.

A retired scallop captain once defined the fishery as "slavery without a whip." All of the *Adventurer*'s crew agreed that almost any other kind of fishing is easier but scalloping is where the money is right now. Most of the crew started fishing one thing or another when they were in their teens and have known little else. Most, including the captain, have only an elementary school education and, therefore, have few options to make comparable wages ashore. In a good year, such as 1986, Frost can make $60,000 to $80,000, and the crew around $30,000 for 100 days at sea. They are deceptive figures, quoted on level ground, far from a deck that on a good day rocks in a 20-degree arc, and is buffeted by a 30-knot breeze which dumps water down your neck when you are picking and shoots spray into your face when you are shucking. At the end of the day, you fall into a narrow bunk in the ship's forecastle.

To a man the crew believe that they earn every penny. "People ashore think we got an easy job, lots of money. But they would be shocked at what we do," one of them said. "Sure, we're six months on the water but you do twelve months work. And you're away from your wife and children. It's hard, hard on everyone." "In most jobs there is a rising and falling rhythm, times when you work at top speed and times when you coast," another observed. "Not so in scalloping. Everything's a mad rush. It takes its toll. The money is good but by the time you're thirty-five, you're through. Look around, they're all young fellows."

The frantic business of icing away scallops continued around the clock. After the *Cygnus* had passed our stern, heading south along the line to show the Maple Leaf to the American boats, Frost ordered the drags pulled as he didn't want to be caught fishing over the line. It was the only time during the days that I was to spend on *Adventurer II* when the drags were deliberately idle. But not for long: the *Cygnus* passed, Frost took one last look at the Americans, and then wheeled to starboard. As he did, he shouted through the open wheelhouse window to the deck crew who had been enjoying the brief and rare respite, "Okay, boys, let's make some money." The horn sounded, a maul was swung, and the drags shot away.

NORTH OF NAIN

In the high-riding bow of the 18-foot speed boat, feet planted resolutely apart and holding hard to the painter, is Abraham "Aba" Kojak, a 50-year old Labrador Inuit fisherman. At the back of the boat is Aba's son, Jacko, gunning the outboard motor as you might expect any 19-year old would do — for all it's worth — so that the boat rides off the ramp of each wave crest, then slams into its deep trough, shooting sharp slivers of pain through my back and neck muscles. I sit huddled in the middle, watching as father and son pass finely tuned signals between one another. Without trying to shout instructions over the sounds of the motor and the boat's pounding, or resorting to hand signals, Aba directs Jacko where to steer and when to alter course. He accomplishes these commands, with a slight, almost imperceptible, nod of his head, to port or starboard.

Jacko responds by cutting around the end of Blow Hard Island. As he does a flock of black guillemots splutters into flight exposing their bright coral-red feet. As the bracing air whips my face, I take in the unfamiliar sights of the northern waters. Several hundred yards to starboard, there are two grounded icebergs. One looks remarkably like a country church, with its single spire at one end and an oval window eroded by wind and water through the other. The bergs shine as if lit from inside, brightening an otherwise melancholy seascape. Suddenly, directly ahead of us, a minke whale surges to the surface, spouts and disappears. "Grumpus," notes Aba, applying the local name for the small rorqual. Over top the barren mound of Blow Hard Island, which is grey and cracked as an elephant's hide, loom the snow-capped, serrated peaks of the Kiglapait Mountains, reflecting the pinkish light of the sun rising from the pewter-coloured Labrador Sea.

Jacko eases off on the throttle, to my relief, and we ride on the chop to check the nets anchored to the lee shore. As the landwash pitches and tosses our small boat, a deep sound reverberates across the water, disturbing the profound quietude of this subarctic wilderness and seeming to vibrate my very ear bones. My first thought is, "Sonic boom from a NATO low level flying exercise." Aba looks up from his net, cocks his head to one side and says, in his perfunctory way: "Iceberg breaking up." Sure enough, on our return to Cut Throat Harbour, I note that my "country church" iceberg, warmed by the mid-summer sun, has split into two pieces. This event provided the first of many occasions for me to marvel at how intimately Inuit like Aba know or, perhaps it is no exaggeration to say, communicate with the land. During the week I am to spend on this remote island, I will often pause to contemplate the coastal landscape of glacial peaks and low granite islands capped with tundra — at once exhilarating and intimidating in their austere grandeur — and to reflect on how the Inuit have survived here for centuries, so effectively that archaeologist William Fitzhugh of the Smithsonian Institution wrote: "It seems impossible to find a spot which has not been modified in some tangible way by Inuit hands."

Though Jacques Cartier never ventured as far as northern Labrador, ironically, his notorious epithet, "the land God gave to Cain," has often been invoked to describe the coast. It is useful, if only to invoke the emotional impact of the landscape, which can inspire a shudder in someone from more equable climes. In many places, wind has stripped the white granite to the bone; elsewhere a few patches of yellowish green turf have been able to establish themselves in the interstices of stone. And even in August acres of snow cling to the north-facing slopes. To a Euro-Canadian such a land might appear so utterly worthless it deserved a rebuke from God.

This transparently ethnocentric view does not take into account either the diverse resources of this outwardly inhospitable environment or the skills that the Inuit have devised to exploit them. For the Labrador Inuit the ocean has always been the prime source of sustenance here — whales, seals, fish and seabirds abound in the icy waters of the Labrador Sea. But the land, too, has been a good provider, for herds of caribou migrate to and from the coast, and other animals and plants contribute to the Inuit diet in season.

The barren islands and deep fjords of the northern Labrador coast, a remote region stretching nearly 500 kilometres from Nain to the Arctic Circle, have been the Inuit homeland for much of their long occupation of Labrador. Glowered over by the highest mountain ranges east of the Rockies, the Kiglapaits and the Torngats, which rise precipitously from the sea, it is one of the last wild frontiers in North America and is unpopulated for most of the year. However, as soon as the ice leaves the coast in late June or early July, Inuit families — grandparents to infants — return to the land of their forebears to engage in the fishery for arctic char and Atlantic salmon. The fishery is the mainstay of the Inuit economy but life in summer fishing camps is also a matter of cultural survival. It is in the camps that the children learn by watching their mothers and fathers how to survive on the land as their ancestors have done for millennia.

As fall announces itself, often with a blustery September gale off the Labrador Sea, Inuit like Aba Kojak move south again to Nain, which is Labrador's most northerly permanent settlement. For many, it is a reluctant transition from a world in which traditional skills suffice to a world dominated by southern values. "I like it here better than in Nain," Andrew Kojak, Aba's 23-year old son, told me at Cut Throat. "Too much money problems in Nain. Around here we can just live off the land." Another Cut Throat fisherman, Alec Dicker, echoed Andrew's sentiments: "I'd rather be here than in Nain," he told me. "Hard on money, hard on yourself. Lot of trouble in them big old communities."

Canada's north has undergone drastic change in the 20th century, and northern Labrador has been no exception. At the turn of the century, there were five permanent settlements north of Nain — Killinek, Ramah, Hebron, Okak and Nutak — reaching to the very tip of northern Labrador. However, in the late 1950s, the triumvirate of power in northern Labrador, namely the Moravian Mission, the International Grenfell Association and the Government of Newfoundland, decided to resettle residents of the two remaining northern communities, Hebron and Nutak, to Nain and Hopedale. Nain, once situated midway in an unbroken string of coastal communities, thus became the most northerly, and the biggest, permanent settlement in Labrador.

Nain is tucked into the head of a deep bay 400 kilometres by air from Goose Bay. Flanked by imposing grey hills, it enjoys a pleasingly dramatic setting. But its reputation as a place afflicted by poverty, social violence and poor sanitary conditions precedes it. Happy kids playing in the sandy streets, where a stranger is sure to receive a friendly greeting, help to distract attention from but cannot mask such Third World problems as communal water supplies, open sewers and makeshift housing. At the centre of town is the fish plant, Nain's economic hub, and across the way is Nain Church. On top of the quaint steeple is a vane stamped with the date 1771 — the year the Moravians (Unitas Fratrum), a German Protestant Missionary sect, succeeded in extending its work from Greenland to the coast of Labrador by establishing their first mission-cum-trading post here.

The Moravians exerted powerful control on the economic life of Labrador for 200 years, but today, even though in Nain you can hear an Inuit brass band, replete with horns, violins and cellos, play baroque music at Christmas and Easter, their influence on day-to-day life has diminished considerably.

As one external influence waned, others swept over northern Labrador. World War II and the Cold War that followed saw the construction of a U.S. Airbase in Goose Bay and radar stations elsewhere along the coast, which lured Inuit off the land into a wage-earning economy — a trend abetted by resettlement in the 1950s. However, the Labrador Inuit now face the greatest challenge that they have yet encountered to their way of life. The deterioration of the fishery in the 1980s, coincident with the loss of the seal pelt market, has resulted in "a level of social and cultural disruption not previously known [on the coast] and unmatched in other areas of the province or nation," according to a 1986 Royal Commission Report on Renewable Resource Use and Wage Employment in the Economy of Northern Labrador.

The social statistics bear out this grim assessment. Infant mortality rates are one-and-a-half to three times higher in Labrador than in Newfoundland; Inuit children suffer a high incidence of skin diseases and ear infections; half of all school children have a bout of tuberculosis; and alcohol abuse is rampant among the adult population.

Perhaps no statistic is more disturbing than that related to suicide. The rate of Inuit suicide in northern Labrador is three times that for native populations nationally, and five times the average rate for the Canadian population as a whole. Particularly discouraging is the fact that most victims are young, 15 to 24; in this age group the suicide rate is 17 times the national average. "They are screams of desperation," says Commission Report author, Carol Brice-Bennett, who relates these numbing statistics to the breakdown of traditional cultural values and, at the same time, an absence of economic opportunities in the northern communities.

I understood that the social problems, so pervasive in Nain, virtually disappeared when people returned to their summer fishing camps. In order to see the more traditional, and happier, side of Inuit life on the land, with the permission of the provincial Department of Fisheries, I booked passage aboard the collector boat, *The Setting Sun*, which ferries fish, families and supplies back and forth between the camps and Nain.

It is a 10-hour, 150-kilometre passage, along some of the most spectacularly scenic coastline anywhere. On the Labrador coast the Canadian Shield meets the North Atlantic — two titanic forces seemingly in conflict. The jagged prominences of the Kiglapait Mountains (Kiglapait means "saw-toothed" in Inuktitut) rise magnificently, 3000 feet from the water line, like great sea fortresses erected against the sea's batterings. After a mercifully calm run (on my first trip to the Labrador coast, seven years before, I had been caught in a frightful gale off Cape Kiglapait), we arrived at Cut Throat (Sillutalik) at dusk. Aba came aboard for a chat with captain Chesley Webb and to pick up his expected visitor. Recognizing that I must be him, he offered his hand: "Don't be lonely, boy. Don't be lonely," he said by way of introduction, his deeply-lined face cracking open with a wide grin.

Once onshore Jacko and two younger boys, Joshua and Gus, eagerly helped me set up my tent. Dispensing with tent pegs, which would have found little soil over the ungiving rock anyway, they anchored my tent as the Inuit have always done, with the generous granite rocks scattered over the island tundra.

"How do you like living in camp?" I asked in the manner of a southerner on a sojourn at a public camping ground.

"This isn't a camp," Jacko corrected me. "This is my home." Jacko was right. Northern Labrador has been "home" to his people for a very long time. Paleo-Eskimos of the Pre-Dorset culture were in northern Labrador four thousand years ago. Ancestors of the present day Inuit belonged to the Thule culture, a highly sophisticated people with origins in the western arctic. They spread into northern Labrador, 700 years ago, from eastern Baffin Island by way of Resolution Island and the Button Islands, appropriately called Tutjat, or "stepping stones." The Thule quickly moved southward into the rich whale-hunting regions between Killinek and Saglek, in the process replacing the resident Dorset culture, which did not have the technology to capture whales or to fully exploit other marine resources. By the late eighteenth century, these adroit and spirited maritime people had occupied the coast of Labrador from its tip at Cape Chidley to Hamilton Inlet.

Travelling the coast, today, it quickly becomes apparent that northern Labradoreans are a mixed race. There are pure blooded Inuks, the Inuit; the Kablunangajuit, or "not quite whites" in Inuktitut; and the "Kabalanks" or whites, sometimes called Settlers. (There are also the Innu of Montagnais-Nascapi origin who live in the coastal community of Davis Inlet.) Sandra Gwyn used the apt analogy, "Pitcairn Islanders," to describe northern Labradoreans. Ninety per cent of northern Labradoreans claim some Inuit heritage and, admirably, Inuit and Kablanangajuit see themselves as one people bound as much by lifestyle as bloodline. A single organization, the Labrador Inuit Association (LIA), reflects this mutual respect, by representing all 4000 native Labradoreans of Inuit extraction. Success in Labrador has always depended, and still does, on a high degree of co-operation among people. That they share their resources and help each other out — unquestioningly, it seems — are the lessons that a harsh land has taught its inhabitants.

The Labrador Inuit have always concentrated their activities on the coastal islands and at the mouths of bays, where they could intercept the arctic char as they migrated toward their spawning rivers, and Atlantic salmon as they moved north along the coast in late summer.

Aba has been coming to Cut Throat Island since 1971. Like most Inuit fishermen Aba brings his family when he comes north to fish. Aba's youngest son Jacko mans the boat with him; two older boys, Kelly and Andrew, have their own boat; another son, the eldest, fishes independently in Okak Bay. Two younger boys, grandson Joshua and adopted son Gus, help out onshore, washing the fish and packing them in ice. Andrew has brought his own family, wife Dora and their 5-month old daughter, Eva — so that three genera-

174

tions live together under one roof, the rule rather than the exception in northern Labrador where the extended family still holds sway. Aba's wife Louisa looks after the household, happily leaving behind the modern conveniences of Nain for the more traditional lifestyle of Cut Throat, where she washes clothes by hand and cooks on a stove fashioned from an oil barrel: "I'd live here all year round if it was up to me. I hope we can always live this way," Louisa says.

The nine-member Kojak family comfortably shares the cramped quarters of a one-room shanty, spartanly appointed with crude bunks cushioned by caribou skin mattresses and a table where the family eats and wiles away evenings playing Scrabble and Yahtzee under a single light bulb powered by a gasoline generator. "It's so peaceful here, except for that generator," Louisa says.

Aba stays in touch with Nain by means of a battery operated shortwave radio. Through the Nain Fish Plant he can place orders for sugar, flour, salt, tobacco (the northern staples); as well, the Fish Plant calls him regularly to check on the weather, the amount of fish they can expect and to see if he needs more ice.

I quickly acquired the moniker "Harry Kablanak" on Cut Throat Island. This alliterative pun (note the "K" in "Kablanak" is pronounced like "H") poked fun both at my appearance, bearded and bushy haired, and my own obvious roots. I took the ribbing as a sign of Aba's acceptance, and soon found myself welcomed into family life on Cut Throat.

Daily routines revolved around checking the nets, first thing in the morning and again in the late afternoon. Aba always carried a rusted shotgun in the bottom of the boat, for every excursion on the water is also an opportunity to put meat on the table. "We have to hunt. We have to have something to eat. No refrigerators in Cut Throat, boy," Aba explained one day, after he had taken an unsuccessful crack at a flock of overflying geese. One morning when the sea was taut as silk, on returning to shore he observed: "Lots of seals this morning."

"Did you get one?" I asked.

"No, can't eat old seal meat all the time."

The Kojak men often spent the afternoons mending nets that had been torn up by grounded icebergs or, as happened this spring, by roving polar bears which had drifted south on the ice. The children wiled away time by fishing barehanded for "baby sculpins" in the tidepools, or roving the tundra in search of lemmings to provision a pair of pet, unfledged rough-legged hawks. The women, meanwhile, tried to keep up with the round of washes and meals. "Always something to do in Cut Throat," observed Louisa, who professes not to miss the amenities of her Nain home.

Perhaps the hardest thing for a Kablanak like myself to learn is patience in conversation. While Aba mended nets, I punctuated the silence with questions. Answers were often slow in coming and, I discovered, might arrive, extemporaneously, the next day. So I learned about the effect of the sealskin ban on Inuit life in Labrador. "No price on sealskins," Aba offered. "Not worth nothing. Greenpeace is a hard crowd. They want us to live on potatoes."

I was impressed by the calmness displayed by Aba, a kind of measured response to life, which perhaps had something to do with the harsh realities of survival on the coast. "It's hard to live on the Labrador," he told me. "Always living off the land. That's our life. We eat seal meat, deer meat, birds, partridges, pigeon eggs...."

One evening Aba showed unusual animation, when, from his cabin window, he watched a hunting party arrive back from a trip to Hebron. "Lots of deers," he said, excitedly, when he saw the caribou lashed to the bow of the boat. The next morning I arrived at the cabin to find the family gathered around a leg of fresh caribou.

Dora was chopping a roast into pieces for the stew pot, but each of the men, including young Gus and Joshua, had his own knife and was helping himself to a portion of the burgundy-coloured meat. Aba seemed to relish the fat in particular. When he noticed my interest, he said with characteristic humour: "You can tell people Aba eats everything raw in Cut Throat, even sculpins."

He handed me his knife to try a piece for myself. "Small piece," he cautioned. "Don't make yourself sick."

Everyone in the family contributed to the supply of "country food" as wild game is called. Even young Gus caught two unfledged ptarmigan one day for the stew pot. With every meal, there was *baniksiak*, an unleavened bread that Louisa whipped up by the dozen in a frying pan.

Summer is a busy time as everyone is putting food by for the long winter ahead. Aba's neighbours, after sharing fresh meat with everyone, began drying what was left. I watched as a woman cut the meat into thin strips with sure strokes of her moon-shaped *ulu*. She then hung up the meat to dry on squares of fishing net suspended on poles. This curing method, similar to the traditional sun-curing of cod, will yield a product, called *kikkuk*, that will keep for two to three months. Also hanging nearby like brightly coloured socks were arctic char. Each fish had been split, then scored crosswise every few inches. After smoking for 24 hours, it is dried for two more days to make *piksik*, a chewy, earthy-tasting delicacy. On a nearby beach rock, a hunter had unceremoniously perched a caribou head, sporting a magnificent set of velvety phase antlers. Jacko cut off the tip of one of the antler prongs, peeled back the velvety covering, and, with the point of his knife, fished out a piece of pale yellow marrow, which he offered to me. At first I politely refused this local delicacy, but, in the end, I relented to his persistence and nibbled on a corner. It was salty and chewy like a toffee; however, I ate only half and surreptitiously let the rest drop to the beach. "We'll make an Inuk of you yet, before you go back to Kablanak land," joked Jacko.

Coming from Kablanak land, I was surprised by the extent to which the Inuit of northern Labrador did subsist off the land. So-called "country food" contributes significantly to the regional economy; in fact, it is the single most important source of income along the coast. As well, country food is an important factor in the health and social well-being of Labradoreans, according to a study by Memorial University of Newfoundland's Faculty of Medicine.

The Labrador Inuit Association was formed in 1973 with the clear objective of maintaining a way of life in which hunting, fishing and trapping continued to be of prime importance. Life in the communities still centres around these traditional pursuits, even though people only relocate to camps during summer. Snowmobiles and speed boats have made it possible for hunters to use the traditional, family-based hunting areas but to continue to live in communities like Nain. Exploitation of species changes from season to season. In summer people primarily pursue char and salmon; in fall they hunt seals and migratory waterfowl; in winter, caribou; and in spring, seals, fish, migratory birds and caribou all contribute to the subsistence economy. Black bears, rabbits, hares and porcupines are hunted as well, and fur-bearing animals are trapped.

As important as subsistence hunting and the food fishery are, the Inuit of northern Labrador have long been engaged in a cash economy as commercial fishermen. In fact, the Labrador Inuit are unique among northern aboriginal groups in Canada, for they have been actively engaged in a commercial fishery of one kind or another for more than 200 years — first for seals, then cod, and since the 1960s char and salmon.

In the last decade the cash economy — and the family life that depends upon it — has been undermined by loss of the seal pelt market, but even more significantly, by declining arctic char stocks in the Nain and Okak Bay areas.

The latter problem can be traced to resettlement, which irrevocably changed northern Labrador, displacing families, disrupting harvest practices, in effect, upsetting the whole economy based on the commercial fishery and subsistence hunting. In the 30 years since resettlement, Nain's population more than doubled to 1100, putting intense pressure on the thinly distributed subarctic resource base, in particular the fish stocks in Nain Bay and nearby Okak Bay.

One day as Aba and Jacko and I were setting out a new net on the back of Cut Throat Island, Aba said: "Used to be a lot of char around here until the end of August. Not any more.

"Ten years there's not going to be nothing around here, maybe in five years time. No char, no nothing."

He paused and breathed out heavily: "If we lose the fishing people will go on welfare. Nothing else we can do."

Inuit fishermen in Northern Labrador face a number of problems peculiar to Labrador, Aba explained. First the season is shortened due to ice, which makes it practically impossible for Inuit fishermen to get the minimum 10 weeks necessary to qualify for unemployment insurance. The federal government has so far refused to adjust the Unemployment Insurance regulations to take the harsh weather conditions of northern Labrador into account. As a result, Inuit fishermen find themselves without an income in the spring when they most need it. "UIC cuts off May 15 and fishing starts June 15," says Aba. "It's really hard when we got to get ready for fishin', no money in the pocket. And we can't get credit for to go fishing. You can hardly make a living these days." To make matters worse, the provincial Fisheries Loan Board has been reluctant to bankroll the purchase of bigger boats by Inuit fishermen, which would allow them to diversify into the offshore ground fishery. So, the Inuit of Labrador find themselves caught in a bureaucratic Catch-22: no money and no credit without money.

We secured the net to a rocky point and pushed off. Aba pointed behind me to the great mauve eminence of Cape Mugford rising in dramatic steps to its glacier-capped peak: "When I was eleven, I lost my uncle through the ice, seal hunting near that big high peak."

"What did you do?" I asked naively.

"I walked back home to Nutak, 15 miles," he said matter-of-factly.

There was a moral in this story — at least for me. I realized that survival for Aba's people now depends as much on their ability to win battles with government to secure access to, and management of, the resources of the coast as on the skills passed from one generation to another. Aba reluctantly recognizes this fact, and for this reason when he leaves Cut Throat, he will return to the LIA office in Nain. Aba is chairman of the local Fisheries and Wildlife Committee (Omajunik kamajet) and also a Land Claims negotiator for LIA. It means travelling to Ottawa and St. John's. "It's hard to leave home when you got to look out for a large family," he says. And, he admits, for a man who grew up in a community (Nutak) where there was no school, no wildlife officer, no RCMP, and everyone spoke Inuktitut, it is hard to deal with bureaucrats. But it is work that he feels compelled to do, if his sons are to have a chance to live off the land as he has done.

"It is hard to go back into the office," he told me, "I don't want to but I have to."

It has taken ten years just for the LIA to get to the negotiating table with the federal and provincial governments (which they finally did in 1988). During this time their economic position has deteriorated markedly, so that they are entering negotiations in an atmosphere of urgency. "People here can't afford any delays," Judy Rowell, Environmental Advisor to the LIA told me. "The erosion of the economy and of the lifestyle is the most serious threat they've got right now."

Recently, the LIA and both levels of government signed an agreement, committing all parties to a resolution of the claim by 1994. Central to the Labrador Inuit claim is their attempt to secure priority rights to the fishery adjacent to the coast. LIA claims that the fishery has been and still is the backbone not only of their economy but of their culture, too. "Cash income is essential for an Inuk," an LIA brief to the Senate Standing Committee on Fisheries states unequivocally. "Without cash an Inuk has no rifle, no ammunition, no fishing gear, no transport, no fuel and no meaningful occupation."

The Labrador Inuit claim that their aboriginal "right to fish" applies not only to coastal waters but to landfast ice (which may extend 20 kilometres offshore) where Inuit hunt seals in winter and spring.

The Inuit now enjoy exclusive access to salmon and char in waters adjacent to their coast, but they also want priority rights to northern cod stocks, for which they currently have no quota. LIA maintains that they do not want to exclude fishermen from the island of Newfoundland, who have been coming to Labrador to engage in the summer fishery for generations; they simply want first crack at the groundfish stocks. It is sure to prove a contentious issue in the land claims debate.

For now, Aba and his fellow fishermen want a faster and bigger collector boat that would allow them to return to the northern fjords of Nachvak and Saglek, where char stocks are healthier. Their requests have been met with silence, however. "Government is hard, especially the province," says Aba. "They don't want to give you nothing."

Pushing the summer fishery north is essential, if the traditional Inuit lifestyle is to survive. LIA has stated its ultimate goal is to re-establish a permanent presence in the far north, probably at Saglek where there is a DND airstrip from which fresh char could be flown to markets in Montreal and New England.

I wondered whether this would ever happen, whether the people themselves — young people especially — wanted to return to the far north to live year round. My brief time on Cut Throat Island had convinced me of one thing: Labrador Inuit need to maintain their way of life in the summer fishing camps, where people work together for the welfare of the family and neighbours, without the interference of institutions ensconced in Nain. On the land — harsh, lonely and challenging as it may seem to someone like me — people have a sense of belonging and of being in control of their own destiny. Contemplating this, I flashed on the image of Aba Kojak in the bow of his boat — resolute and unshakeable — guiding his son through the familiar, home waters of the Labrador Sea.

THE DEVIL'S WORK IS AN ARK OF SAND

"There she is, there's your island." Thus did my cabin mate, Russ Miller, greet me on a June morning. For 12 hours, the Canadian Coast Guard vessel, *William Alexander,* had beat across the riled sea; now she lay uneasily at anchor. I peered sleepily through the porthole. The sky was grey; the Atlantic, the colour of a heavier metal. In between was an incongruous slip of white land, Sable Island. My island? I suppose it is, technically. I am a Nova Scotian, and this place — to me, until that moment, more fabled Avalon than real domain — has been Nova Scotia's easternmost territory since the province first established life-saving stations there in 1803. Whoever may claim it, Sable still belongs to the North Atlantic first, and to Maritime history, because it has been so voracious in its appetite for men and ships, rising from the waters where no land should be.

What was it doing here, one hundred miles from the nearest landfall of peninsular Nova Scotia? "The devil's work," wrote onetime Sable wireless operator, Thomas Raddall, in his novel, *The Nymph and the Lamp.* Perversely, Sable sits in the middle of the North Atlantic's busiest shipping lanes, where until the invention of radar it regularly renewed its right to the notorious epithet, "Graveyard of the Atlantic." Geologically, it is a relic of the Ice Age, 1000 metres of sand deposited by the retreating glacier 10,000 years ago. Most of that thick blanket of sand is now a submerged fishing bank, which made fortunes for some sons of Gloucester and Lunenburg but cruelly harvested others. Sable, the island, is an emergent promontory. Its unlikely latitude-longitude (44 degrees N, 60 degrees W) is near the convergence of the Gulf Stream and the Labrador Current. However, this seems to be mere coincidence.

It is a local and tidally-generated current, spiralling around the island, that actually holds it in place against the tireless battering of the waves. Its rhythmic dunes is the work of the wind, blowing at 25 knots from the northeast when I arrived. A beach craft, which looked like war surplus from D-Day, was being used to ferry 3,000-gallon tanks of gasoline to the weather station, an outpost of Canada's Atmospheric Environment Service. Taking into account the surf, I opted for a dry-footed landing by helicopter.

One must have an express purpose for setting foot on Sable and the blessing of the Canadian Coast Guard, the island's jealous guardian. Sable is seasonal home to those who do research on fisheries, oceans and wildlife and to various provincial and federal officials, all charged with overseeing this sandbar's flora, fauna and residents. In recent years oil drillers have plumbed the sands, and occasionally writers like myself have come to plumb Sable's less tangible treasures. I was the guest of the Canadian Wildlife Service and stayed with seabird biologist Tony Lock at his small hut near the east end of the 22- mile-long crescent.

Sable has an abrupt way of impressing certain verities upon its transients. The cycle of decay from birth to death seems fore-shortened here, perhaps only because it is so glaringly obvious. Evidence is everywhere on the ground, as I discovered on my first walk. I kept to the better worn wild horse paths to avoid the nesting ground of terns. They seemed unimpressed by my care. Wisely mistrustful of any intruder, however well-intentioned, they swooped overhead and raised a screed of protest at my approach. Gulls, an ever-present threat to the terns, nest here too. I found four spotted gull's eggs in a nest constructed of dried marram grass and horse dung, the two most available building materials — one, after all, is the other in different form.

A little further on, I nearly stumbled upon a dishevelled horse carcass, flaps of reddish hide draped over the skeleton as over the wire frame of a mannequin. The nose and eyes were gone. Softparts of animals disappear quickly on Sable but in the absence of large predators all else is achingly persistent. In the days ahead I become accustomed to the remains of seabirds, seals, whales and horses. Sable had begun to wrap a cowl of sand around this victim. It is constantly covering, then disinterring its prey, a fact which was distressing to its inhabitants in the 19th century, when the dead were often sailors thrown ashore by the sea's violence.

The East Light blinked its warning over the top of a high dune. I headed in the direction of this landmark, again unprepared for what I found over the rise. There was a weathered house, three-quarters buried. I slid down the slope of the dune, and, stooping, entered by an upstairs window. The bedroom closet was nearly full of sand, the door casually ajar. I crawled to avoid bumping my head on the lintel. As I entered the upstairs hall, the damp, chilling breath of the house rose up the open back staircase. It was suddenly dark and unsettling. For a moment, I considered easing myself into the bowels of this entombed house. However, I had no light, and my courage abandoned me completely when a bird suddenly burst from a back bedroom and bucked out a window. I retreated, leaving the spirits of the house to rest, and wended my way back to camp, eager to share my discoveries. Dick Brown, pelagic seabird biologist, informed me that he had slept in the same house in 1970. On Sable, sand as the measure of time has a poignant everyday relevance.

Tony Lock was fond of saying, "On Sable you live the slimmed down life." Long walks become my daily regimen. I wandered the landscape (aimlessly as the horses, it seemed) foraging for flotsam, which is everywhere. All glass is exquisitely sandblasted. Even the most mundane item, such as a Pepsi bottle, has a misty charm after Sable's sands, driven by North Atlantic winds, have had a few weeks to work on it. The dunes are difficult terrain, not the least because the dry sand gives way at each step. I soon came to prefer the more compacted sand of the beach, even though this more dynamic environment was not as rich in artifacts. However, every several hundred yards, there were herds of twenty or more harbour seals and their pups. (Sable is Atlantic Canada's largest harbour seal breeding ground.) Their dish-shaped faces with inscrutable coal-black eyes would bob up from the surf, and I was always accompanied by one or more of these curious creatures. On my second day, one hauled out for a closer look before bustling back into the sea. This almost human, beckoning behaviour made me feel that it was expecting me to follow, to assume its likeness, become a sleek form with flippers.

Each day, my companions — Lock and Brown and Canadian Wildlife Service biologist Colleen Hyslop — used a rocket net to catch immature Common and Arctic terns which seemed content to spend most of their time loafing on the beach. The adult males, on the other hand, frantically foraged out to sea, returning with silver sandlances in their bright coral beaks for prospective mates. Late in the afternoon of the third day, we too decided to make a foray away from camp. We hopped on our bikes and headed for the East Bar, the three-mile spit of barren sand that is one end of Sable. The green sea was driven ashore on a southeast wind, the breakers advancing over the bars which run parallel to the island and were the nemesis of so many ships. The further we went east, the darker, colder and more melancholy the day became. Seemingly in sympathy with the worsening weather, the bar itself became utterly barren, except for the tiny disasters which had converged there. When I visited, Sable's shores were littered with all sizes of new lumber. The wood, I learned, had been carried on the Gulf of St. Lawrence current as it swept around the edge of Cape Breton. Like hay in a haystack, the boards stuck out of the sand at every angle. Old tree trunks, worn smooth, and oil rig refuse added clutter. And there was the usual carnage: a seal fatally wounded by a shark bite. Among this unremarkable refuse was a forty-foot section of a nineteenth-century top-gallant mast. Cracked and weathered, it nevertheless bespoke the grandeur of the ship which like 500 others had met its end on Sable's shores.

We maneuvered through the rubble to the tip of the bar, where we were greeted by a great herd of grey seals. Three thousand grey, white and buff lozenges of fat lumbered into the crashing sea as we bore down on them. The fleeing seals left the air rancid in their wake. In January and February, the scene must be even more impressive — as must be the stench. Then, herds of 20,000 and more frequent Sable's bars: 12,000 breeders, 6,000 pups and as many as 4,000 non-breeders.

If reminders of death are everywhere on Sable, one realizes that he is also in the midst of great fecundity. Anytime I cast my eye around, seals were feeding in the waters or sunning on the beach; horses were feeding in the marram or galloping beside the surf; seabirds were filling the air with shrill sound. Sable is sanctuary as well as graveyard. Oppressive in light of human history, it is nevertheless a majestic natural place.

As we turned for home, the sun broke through the cobalt sky. The whole complexion of the bar was suddenly transformed.

Minutes before it had been a dreary expanse; now it seemed to shine with inner light. We came across a grey seal pup with a piece of green fishing net tangled tightly round its neck. Using a flexible piece of one-by-three lumber as a teeter-totter and the seal as a fulcrum, Colleen and I pinned the frightened animal. It hissed like a cat and showed its formidable row of curved teeth as Lock cautiously cut the net free. We continued on, our spirits lifted by our own act of samaritanism and the ever-strengthening light that now bathed the whole island — a green and white moon shape curving into a sea rich with life.

Like the weather, one's mood changes suddenly on Sable, moment to moment, from one day to another. The next day I found myself, unaccountably, restless and anxious. I mentioned this to Dick Brown, who has undergone many long voyages. He recognized the syndrome. Three days afloat, the exhilaration wears off. It begins to set in that you're trapped, there's nowhere to go.

Sable, an Ark of sand, has its unique fauna. Perhaps the best known is the Sable Island horse. Horses were probably first introduced by Andrew LeMercier, a Boston clergyman, who tried to colonize the island in the early 18th century. Today the Sable Island horse is considered a breed apart and is one of only a few wild populations on the planet. But wild seems too strong a word to describe these creatures, which have reversed the usual trend toward domesticity. They are stoic, doleful, and to a degree, sociable — perhaps the less inflammatory term "feral" suits them better. After several days it occurred to me that I had not heard so much as a whinny out of them. They roam the island in small, discrete herds of families or bachelors. We had our resident group, which was somewhat non-conformist: three scraggly stallions and an unusually sleek chestnut mare. Occasionally they stopped by to scratch their ragged hides against our thin-walled shack or to crop the marram. I responded to a commotion outside one day, to find Lock muttering: "Eating my grass. They cause all these blow-outs."

Marram, with its tessellation of deep roots, holds the island together. Men and horses have disturbed this finely knit fabric, however, making the island more vulnerable to the force of storms which regularly sweep over it. Barrier dunes are breached, the bars shift, the island's interior is gouged out. In fact, the shape and dimensions of Sable have altered significantly as can be seen from

185

a comparison of early and contemporary surveys of the island. A reliable map by Joseph Des Barres in 1776 shows a major lagoon in the interior of the island. Wallace Lake, as it was called, remained navigable from the sea until late in the 19th century. Now it is much diminished in size and entirely landlocked.

Fortunately, the island has its own underground lens of fresh water, and the wind, however fierce, can only remove the sand to the water table. Our well was located at the bottom of a blow-out behind Tony Lock's shack. The hand pump was mounted on a platform out of reach of the horses, which also used the blow-out as their water source. One day when I went for water, I found them digging their own well with their front hooves, pawing away the sand to make a shallow depression that quickly filled with water. I returned minutes later to find the horses gone. In their place were two Ipswich sparrows using the horses' well as a bird bath. These pale-grey sparrows, which overwinter on coastal sand dunes in the Central Atlantic States, breed only on Sable.

The well that became a birdbath struck me as an example of domestic co-operation between creatures sharing a small island. As one might expect, cramped co-habitation is not always this compatible. For the terns, which nest in the marram, the relationship with the ever-foraging horses is fundamentally antagonistic. Horses leave broken eggs and trampled chicks behind them.

Lock believes that there has been a drastic decline in the number of Sable terns. Described as immense at the turn of the century, the colony may then have numbered one million individuals and acted as a refugium for the species on the east coast. For at least two hundred years the terns have shared Sable with horses, so it appears their decline to contemporary estimates of 2,500 cannot be attributed primarily to them. More recent immigrants have caused the most havoc. Terns are being heavily depredated by herring gulls and great black-backed gulls, whose population explosion along the entire East Coast has spread even to this most offshore of islands. In Lock's opinion their proliferation at the tern's expense begs some kind of control. The horses, meanwhile, will remain unmanaged and inviolate. They are protected by law, public opinion on the mainland, and the sentiment of any lucky enough to share their island.

Lock pointed out, "Man can't live on an island without wanting to introduce something." The island's earliest colonists introduced cattle, sheep, hogs and, of course, horses. Horses are all that remain of man's attempts to domesticate this Atlantic landscape.

Sable-before-horse must have been a more verdant place. In exclosures around the fisheries research station cabins, the marram grew to luxuriant heights compared to the close cropped grasses elsewhere. Other flora flourishes, however. One of the tern nesting areas is named the Strawberry Colony. When I was there, the ground was awash in the pale blossoms. Parts of the island's interior are generously vegetated while others — such as Bald Dune, at seventy-five feet the island's highest point — are utterly denuded. From its prominence one day, I counted forty-seven of the island's estimated population of 350 horses. This number represents a peak in a cycle which Lock has shown is dictated by the weather. Every seven or eight years, there is an unusually high snowfall on Sable and as many as 100 horses starve to death. The population cycle begins anew.

On the morning of day six, I returned as I had come, holding hard to Lock's all-terrain vehicle as we scooted along the south beach and Wallace Flats (once the site of Wallace Lake). A fixed-wing aircraft was due to land on the beach, but fog, which can wrap the island for days and weeks, descended in earnest. The flight was grounded in Halifax. It was for the best. A mechanical check revealed the tail section was seriously rusted. I was on Sable until another plane could be mustered or a Mobil Oil helicopter came our way. I settled in to see how the other half lived, those for whom Sable was home for months on end.

The manning of Sable is no longer important to ships, which can steer well clear of the island's treacherous shoals. The heart of the island's practical purpose is the Atmospheric Environment Service Station. Sable is one of thirty-three so-called upper air stations in Canada. At each one, theoretically at the same moment, technicians release a hydrogen weather balloon into the atmosphere. This probe of the world's changing weather — nowhere more changeable than on Sable, it seems — is repeated twice daily, at precisely 8:15 a.m. and p.m., Sable time. It is one of two atmospheric events that mark the daily lives of Sable denizens. The other is the overpass of the transatlantic Concorde. Its sonic boom rattles the station windows, jolts you into the day. Paul Workman, the Island's handyman, perhaps best summed up life on Sable: "In a way, it's like a space station here: the work is routine but highly technical, the number of people is limited [six], and each person has a specific purpose for being here."

For each person the island also comes to have a different meaning, which, I was beginning to appreciate, was what my cabinmate had implied the morning I first caught sight of Sable. *Your island, my island* — Sable enters each individual's mythology in a highly personal way.

Near the end of my sojourn I met Sherod Crowell, another highly skilled technician, who helps locate the giant jack-up rigs precisely over their drilling sites, work he had done for a decade. It hadn't taken long for Crowell to fall in love with Sable. "It was August, all the wild roses were in bloom," he recalled. "I've been passing through for a long time. It's like home now." Throughout the 1970s, Sable offshore oil and gas production seemed imminent; now, with cheap oil flowing once again, there were just two rigs still drilling on Sable Bank, and the bank's prospects as an oil producer were dim. For Crowell, this meant a reluctant cutting of ties.

After lunch at Nova Scotia Government House, a modular hut of fibreglass whose entrance is an overarching gate of a whale rib and a ship's rib, Crowell led me to the Rose Bowl, a natural depression rimmed by a profusion of wild rose bushes. It is said the roses were planted by keepers of the old Main Life Saving Station as a memorial to a French ship that went ashore here with great loss of life. We observed an impromptu moment of silence.

Sable provides a welcome opportunity for a person to do some mental beachcombing, collecting memories like flotsam and jetsam. Said Crowell:"I look inside myself a lot, which is not a bad thing. It's a good place to think."

But for Crowell the island was not only a good place to get, and stay, in touch with himself. He had gone beyond mere introspection, confessing that he had come to feel a kinship "with all the lives that have been lived here." Or, for that matter, lost here. Sometimes he had felt something, or someone, as he worked alone at night. There was nothing occult about these encounters with Sable's past spirit. It was an expression of respect for the place, which takes many forms for those willing to open themselves to it.

Now that the oil boom is over, there will be less reason for people to visit the island, to disturb, or commune with, its spirits. Sable can return more to its natural order.

My last afternoon on Sable I gained a glimpse into what that order might be. I checked my impulse to roam and took up a station on a high dune, with a view inland and a prospect of the sea. Shafts of light muscled through the marram grass. A very young foal dozed several yards away, nestled in the long grass, as a herd of seven shaggy, thick-legged Sable horses grazed mindful of but uninhibited by my presence. The water's shadows were aqua and mauve. Fat harbour seals loafed on the north beach while in the shallows mothers passed on to their pups the aquatic acumen of their race. One mother propelled herself on her back, supporting her pup, who swam above her. Rolling, they dived, their heads reappearing in unison. The mother's flipper dunked the pup, and they were off again. All around older pups exploded out of the water, splashing down with adolescent exuberance and showmanship. Further offshore the slow shadows of grey seals feeding: a ponderous ballet. Sable's much maligned land and sea were nurturers that day. I walked back to the Staff House, which was as peaceful as an Edward Hopper painting, remembering what a young weather technician had told me: "When it starts to feel like home here, it is time to leave."

EPILOGUE

Atlantic Canadians do not embrace change. I believe that we may even harbour a kind of ancestral fear of change, for the last time that there was a major upheaval in the status quo, at Confederation, capital and political power shifted away from these shores — and never came back. Be that as it may, there are reasons to distrust change, for its own sake, and I am not alone in my skeptical view of the notion, which to many is the same thing as "progress."

George MacKay Brown, the renowned poet of the Orkney Islands, has described progress in his community of farmers and fisher-folk on the other side of the Atlantic as "a cancer that makes an elemental community look better, and induces a false euphoria, while it drains the life out of it remorselessly." I only have to invoke the resettlement program of outport Newfoundland to know that such an analysis can apply here with equal force.

In considering the recent history of Atlantic Canada, I might as easily invoke the old saw,' The more things change the less things change'. Take the current sorry state of the fishery. In 1983 I spent two months travelling around Newfoundland and Labrador on assignment for *National Geographic*. It was an unsettling time for most Newfoundlanders as deep-sea trawlers were rusting at dockside, the inshore cod fishery had failed again, and whole communities that had survived on "The Rock" since the time of Sir Humphrey Gilbert seemed to be teetering on the brink of extinction. Only Hibernia oil (which remains under the blanket of the Grand Banks) offered a vague hope for a better future.

A massive infusion of public funds into the pockets of multinational fish companies again revived the perennially moribund fishery and induced a short-lived false state of euphoria. Now, a mere seven years later, the fishery is again in crisis and the very companies that benefitted from the government bail-out are threatening to shut down whole communities, including Canso, Nova Scotia, where fishermen first came in 1560.

Another community that the corporations want to cut loose is Gaultois, an outport on Newfoundland's trackless south coast. An image, viewed from the CN ferry, lingers: Gaultois clinging tenuously to the shore, as if by a holdfast, the terrain so steep and rocky that there is not even a place for footpaths let alone roads. Instead there are catwalks constructed on makeshift trestles, which bridge the houses and lead along the cliffside to the fishplant, the town's one industry. The very look of the place bespeaks an extraordinary precariousness and at the same time an almost heroic tenacity.

I travelled onto Francois, midway along the coast. The tiny outport sits at the bottom of a gigantic earth bowl carved out by the retreating glacier. A rockslide, frozen in a geologic moment, seems poised to crush the fragile houses — turquoise, dory yellow, bright green — that are cradled between the wind-scoured land and the wind-tossed sea. It is a hard place where, in order to survive, you must fish from a small boat in all months of the year. However, many prefer the life they have there to what a wider world might offer. As I prepared to return to that world, John Fudge walked me to the ferry. We threaded between the houses on a gravel footpath and on boardwalks like those I had seen in Gaultois. John reflected on life in Francois: "You have your livelihood and you have your freedom. What more can you ask of life?"

What more indeed? However, the livelihood of many small communities in Atlantic Canada — whether it is based on the land, the water or the woods — is threatened. It is threatened not because people there are unproductive, rather because our society has ruthlessly extracted resources from the hinterland and the margins of the country — and then, conveniently, forgotten the source. People in such unfortunate places stand to lose everything: their homes, their savings, even their family and friends. Ultimately, society risks losing a great deal as well. For we are making a decision to sacrifice a value system that is firmly rooted in a sense of individual freedom and, at the same time, is the source of community spirit. Nor should we forget that in the outposts people maintain a working relationship with their environment. To lose that vital connection, and the wisdom it confers, seems folly for us all.

Acknowledgements

The single most gratifying thing about my work as a journalist — and something that never ceases to amaze me — is how freely people invite me into their lives, not, I think, because they seek publicity but because they genuinely wish to be neighbourly to this curious stranger. As an axiom of my travels, it seems that the more remote the location, the more giving people are of their time and resources. I hope that my genuine interest in their lives, expressed in these stories, in some measure compensates them for their kindness.

The author gratefully acknowledges a grant from the Nova Scotia Department of Tourism and Culture which aided in the preparation of this manuscript.

The author also thanks the editors of the magazines which first published these articles. Some appear here in revised form:

Atlantic Insight:
   "End of the Trail," September 1983. (appeared as "Advocate,N.S.")
   "Mining a Thin Seam Wasn't God's Idea," June, 1979

Audubon:
   "The Devil's Work is an Ark of Sand," March, 1989

Canadian Geographic
   "Island Pastoral," June/July, 1990

Equinox:
   "Outport Renaissance," December, 1981
   "Storming the Sand Castles," September/October 1984
   "After the Bump," September/October, 1984
   "The Glory and the Grit," November/December, 1985
   "The Land of Lost Dreams," November/December, 1987
   "Bottom Line," July/ August, 1987

Harrowsmith:
   "The Fat of The Land," February, 1981
   "Prest's Last Stand," August/ September, 1983
   "The Enemy Above," April/May, 1982
   "Of Cabbages and Kings," November/ December, 1986

Yankee Homes:
   "The Elements of Beginning," July, 1988.